Especially for June and Robert Rousey
with all best wishes
for real prosperity

a conversation
with
PETER P. PENCE

Liberty
Apr 28, 1997

BY *David Dick*
DAVID DICK

Price: 1,595 pennies

($15.95)

This Volume is Number *1548/3000*

Signed and Numbered Limited Edition of

A Conversation With Peter P. Pence

First Edition, August, 1995

First Edition, August,1995
Copyright 1995
by
Plum Lick Publishing
1101 Plum Lick Road
Paris, KY 40361-9547

Cover design/illustration and book production
by Stacey Freibert Design

Book illustrations by Jackie Larkins

Back inset photo by Eulalie Dick

Other Books by David Dick

The View from Plum Lick
Follow the Storm
Peace at the Center

ISBN: 0-9632886-3-6

Library of Congress Catalog Card Number
95-92250

for

my mother and father

Lucile Barnes Crouch
1902–1975
and

Dr. Samuel Stephens Dick
1895–1931

FOREWORD

A clear voice to speak of spiritual and material wealth possibly was never more needed than it is today. Whatever occurred yesterday, whatever might happen tomorrow, the time is at hand for diligent prayer and a stronger work ethic coupled with the conservation of the fruits of all honest labor. Such was the simple belief of a fictional man, Peter P. Pence, modeled after many quiet Kentuckians who've lived out their lives in the hush of rural surroundings, mindful of their history, confident in themselves while they lived, hopeful for new generations in centuries to come.

Peter and the other characters in *A Conversation with Peter P. Pence*, with the exception of historical figures, are entirely fictional and any resemblance to living persons, present or past, is entirely coincidental. The name "Peter P. Pence" is derived directly and solely from "Peter's Pence," the 10th-century practice of requiring each householder in England to give a pence to the Church in Rome. There is no intended connection to anyone, living or dead, with the family name of Pence, and any resemblance to any real person, living or dead, is completely coincidental.

The name, "Peter P. Pence," bubbled up from a well-spring of subconsciousness where surely it had been sleeping for decades. Long ago, perhaps, the term Peter's Pence had lodged in the part of my brain reserved "FOR FUTURE USE WHEN ALL ELSE SEEMS TO HAVE FAILED." We would like to think that in the brain, everything is potentially retrievable, and *Peter P. Pence*, in the latter days of the 20th century called out from the depths of universal discourse, called out with an uncommon sense of urgency to be heard.

Peter and I have yearned to make a statement about the importance of individualism, humanitarianism and a close, personal kinship with God.

I wish to thank my soul mate, Eulalie, for her patient understanding of my need.

David Dick
Plum Lick, Kentucky
June 2, 1995

PROLOGUE

I have come to remind you of
our community, of our country,
of our brothers and our sisters
and our relationship to God.

I have come to remind you of
heritage, of self-worth, self-reliance,
dignity
and responsibility.

I say there is no lasting basis
for despair, cynicism
or loss of faith.

I submit there is a far greater
resource of human goodness,
spiritual
and material wealth
in the
United States of America
and throughout the world
than we would ever dare imagine.

I believe it begins with the penny.

Peter P. Pence

CHAPTER ONE

Peter P. Pence lived up the hollow in a log dogtrot on the side of a hill in a remote, rural area called the Pocket, a loop of land formed by the lace of tributaries in the watersheds of the Licking River valleys.

In late 1999, "Old Peter's Peter," as he was derided by some, was 99 years old, born on January 1, 1900, the tenth and last child of Prudence and Patience Pence, who were born in the same dogtrot.

The parents' contemporaneous births had occurred about one year after the final major battle of the Civil War in Kentucky—the Civil War, pitiful and hideous, like a limestone crusher pulverizing good, clean rock.

"Well, well, well," Peter P. Pence boomed in a richly mellowed bass voice, "it's just so good to see you."

His right hand felt firm as he met the movement of Robert Anderson's, made contact with it as quietly and good as a cotton glove in summer. Peter P. Pence would not have considered it mannerly to skimp on a handshake. His smile stretched across his face with a warm and generous expansiveness, his mouth seeming almost pained to open, yet did so as a signal that anything he said should probably be attended carefully, not wasted.

"Mr. Pence, I've come from Atlanta to interview you for the *New York Times*' 21st century issue. I'm honored that you are willing to talk with me," said Robert Anderson in November of 1999.

Pieces of laughter chortled up from the bottom of Peter's lungs, his whole face blending into a compassionate, sincere, unselfish friendliness. His dog was a mixture of black and white merging into splotches of gray, one eye darker than the other, probably Australian shepherd with a dash of border collie. She lay at her master's feet and stared up at him with a look so fixed it seemed as if the dog had died and been immediately subsumed into heaven.

"You have honored me by wanting to come and see a very old man, indeed, possibly among your oldest subscribers, I should imagine?"

"Yes sir, you are certainly among our most loyal readers, but that's only a small part of why I've come to see you."

"I surely was surprised when I received your letter, and I'm pleased that my response reached you. What would you like to talk about, young man?" Peter asked as he lowered himself back into the ancient rocking chair, dropping his right hand down and outward in the direction of the dog's devotion.

"We're in trouble."

"The New York Times is in trouble?"

"The United States of America is in trouble. The world is in trouble too."

"Which includes the New York Times?"

"Includes us all, Mr. Pence."

"Yes, I know. But what I don't understand is why it has taken so long for the nation and the world to wake up to what has happened in the past 200 years. We have fought like hellcats and mad dogs. We have wasted our time and squandered our wealth. And we still lie around complaining about it."

"Is there an answer?"

"There is a remedy, and I believe I know what it is."

"That's the main reason why I'm here, Mr. Pence."

"Remember, there are no quick and easy solutions. Everything worthwhile and of lasting importance comes in a *process* stretched over

time. Please don't come here as most reporters would, then, to gather up a few crumbs of utterances from me to take them to New York to bake them into another mindless pie of self-serving tabloid journalism."

"You have my word that I will listen carefully. Many years ago, the *New York Times* came to a better understanding of the incredible dangers of yellow journalism."

"What does yellow journalism mean to you, Mr. Anderson?"

"It means superficiality. It means sensationalism. Means pandering."

"Means going to hell in a hand basket."

"Yes."

"And although the *Times* has stood head and shoulders above it, we're all ass-deep in it?" added Peter P. Pence.

As the year 2000 approached, Peter P. Pence seemed in reasonably fine fiddle—good health, mind strong—filled with determination to spend his last moments wisely, above all with prudence and patience, his life one day to be remembered as a monument in perpetuity to the two 16-year-old sweethearts, Prudence and Patience Pence, the seed of Jacob and Daniel.

When Robert Anderson came to visit Peter, at last an old man himself, he was seated in the black walnut rocking chair carved and crafted by his father in 1880, the year Peter's ill-fated elder brother, Paul, had been born. The rockers in the back at their tips had worn down to stubbiness.

Prudence, the once beautiful, but strangely bedeviled mother, dead now almost 90 years, had delighted in rocking—back and forth, rocking back and forth—the baby, Paul, his mouth snugly around the ample nipple, mother and child as near total contentment as they'd ever been or ever would be.

The hand-rests in front on the arm pieces of the chair were smooth with the rubbings of Peter P.'s weathered fingers too, especially the thumbs to the inside, along the top edges and across the flat surfaces where he sometimes placed the streaked palms of his aging hands. The hand-rests were also the pivot points of the chair, used as steadying leverage posts by a primeval man to raise his body to a standing position, however unstable it might appear at first sighting. Despite his aging and now fragile heart, Peter P. Pence would not consider it polite to remain seated when a visitor came calling.

His trousers were heavy ribbed corduroy cinched by a wide cowhide belt with a name plate on the left side that read "Peter P. Pence," one of his few concessions to vanity. His wool shirt was a red, black and silvery plaid, buttoned at the top to conserve warmth within and keep cold without.

"I hoped you would share some of your ideas with our other readers, especially how you have accumulated your own wealth, for I understand you are unusually rich," Anderson said, as he sat on a nail keg on the puncheon floor in front of the fire. "Would you like for me to add a lump of coal?"

"Yes, that would be kind of you." Peter's voice followed the reporter over his shoulder. "You seem to understand the importance of adding a bit of fuel while it is still not needed but will be soon enough. There's nothing better than keeping the flames a little ahead of their need. A fire untended will soon turn cold, flicker out as surely as the north wind blows, isn't that right, Pumpkin?" Mr. Pence said, the words sliding smoothly down his right arm to the dog. She raised her head to smile a dog smile, and her docked tail wagged to the tips of its fine-spun tufts of feathers.

Anderson, who had built his career on finding unusual people in little places, doing little things, but receiving little if any recognition for it, finished adding the piece of coal, the flames licking it hotly, causing the jet black anthracite to crackle and spit out hard, clean slivers brittle with fractured age.

"You wish to know how I've accumulated *wealth*? You would like to know what has made me *rich?*" Peter P. Pence sighed, his steel-gray eyes shining as they connected with the reporter.

"Yes, I would."

There was a lengthy, rather unusual pause seeming to last several minutes as Mr. Pence scratched his forehead beneath his weathered hunter's hat. He snapped his right-hand fingers once and Pumpkin raised herself to a sitting position without once taking her eyes from her master. He looked to his right, where books were stacked in shelves from floor to ceiling. It seemed, perhaps, as if the old man were gathering the strength he needed to speak as clearly and carefully and thoughtfully as possible.

"I shall give you the *eleventh* commandment, then," he said as he turned back in Anderson's direction. Pumpkin again lowered her face to her extended paws, the flaking claws taking a purchase on the floor.

"The *eleventh* commandment?" asked Robert Anderson.

"Yes. The first ten are fundamental to right living, and almost all of our troubles begin with the breaking of these great laws, which I have read every Sunday since my mother, Prudence, first introduced me to them when I was seven years old—that was when I believe I attained the age of knowing right from wrong, the time of accepting responsibility for beginning wisdom, don't you see?"

From midway, he rubbed the chair arms outward to the front knobs, drawing in new air and declaring, "I tried my level best to *live* the Ten Commandments as given to Moses by God Almighty. Many of my brothers and sisters seemed to have had more trouble with them. The ten commandments are here in the 20th chapter of Exodus," said Peter P. Pence as he reached to his immediate right, taking a worn, tattered, yellow-paged Bible from the small table there. The page edges were frayed and the front cover was missing. The end cover had begun to peel back upon itself, much as the rearmost part of the rockers on Peter's chair had shortened with continuous use. The Bible had been printed in 1894 by the American Bible Society, "Translated out of The Original Greek."

"One should not consider the possibility of additional commandments without recalling the original ten," said Peter P. Pence with solemn reverence. He closed the Bible, placing a feathered marker at the place of Chapter XX of Exodus, then leaned forward toward Robert Anderson and asked "Now then, young man, have you any idea what the *eleventh* commandment might *be*?"

Robert Anderson looked for a moment at the fire, felt its warmth against his knees and kneading hands between them, then looked back at the old man and said, "I'd like to know."

"The eleventh commandment is: *Thou shalt not spend more than thou earneth.*"

There was another pause as the words hung in the air as certain as the North Star and the six other brightest stars of the Little Dipper above the stately, ancient, silvery sycamore standing tall on the bank of the creek.

"That *sounds* good."

"Yes, and it *is* good."

"We heard others speak often during the early days of debate about the balanced budget amendment," Robert Anderson proffered with a tone of formally educated liberal sagacity. "But permit me to observe that your eleventh commandment might have been timely in its day, but perhaps not in the 11th hour of the present generation with its *unique* requirements."

Peter P. Pence gently sighed again. He looked directly at Anderson and said nothing.

"I mean, Mr. Pence," Anderson began on a slope he knew to be slippery from the top, "yours is really a simplistic idea, ineffective in the resolution of complications within a complex web of personalities and situations."

Mr. Pence placed the nail of his right thumb beneath his lower lip, his forefinger making a "T" across his upper lip. The reporter waited for more words to come. None did.

"Mr. Pence, I did not intend to offend you," Robert Anderson lamely offered, as he unbuttoned the vest of his three-piece suit, a gesture having as much to do with friendliness as it did with the heat of the fireplace. "Would you like me to open up the last lump of coal I added to the fire?"

"Thank you," Peter replied in a voice low and throaty, distinctly resonant, ringed with unmistakable displeasure mixed with soul-turning disappointment, as troubled as a muffled growl, a dog's early warning to a suspicious trespasser in the Pocket.

As Anderson angled the iron poker into the coal and twisted it open, he desperately thought about what he might say next. "The Ten Commandments, regrettably, are seldom lived as you have lived them in your long life, Mr. Pence. Yet still worse, your eleventh commandment has become—I don't know how else to say this—a curse—do you suppose it might be a curse that seems to enjoy mocking us every day of our lives? Perhaps the same thing was at work on the other members of your family."

Robert Anderson drew the question from the pool of conversations he'd had when he'd stopped for a get-acquainted session with county judge executive Lewullen Thomas, a political operative who knew at least something about everybody who'd ever lived in the Pocket. Anderson blurted out the "other members of the family," and instantly wished he'd not referred to the often-murmured tradition in the Pocket that the Pence family long ago had been damned from the outset, brothers fighting brothers, identical twins at that, first cousins marrying first cousins, a mafia murder, triplet stillbirths, twin drunks, and murder and cholera epidemics moving in with what seemed to be an unholy alliance peppered with missionary zeal.

Peter knew that everybody else knew of the Pence family's wrathful story, for there were few secrets in the Pocket, and there'd always been tales to tell, the stranger the better for the telling.

"Young man," said Peter P. Pence, "I suggest that our conversation is finished for today. Neither do I wish to be offensive. You see, I am too old to debate this elemental issue—no, I simply do not *wish* to argue with you. That is all. I am willing to continue our conversation next Sunday at the same time, assuming of course that you would care to return. Perhaps a week of thinking about what I have said to you and what you have said to me will better prepare you for a clearer understanding of the reality that it is *impossible* to spend more than you earn. You may *think* it is possible, and you may spend somebody else's money, but when you do, you deceive at least two people, you and the other person who fell for it. Anybody, whether it was my brother, Poplar, or my brother, Adam, ANYBODY, including County Judge Lewullen Thomas, and especially including the President of the United States, anybody anywhere who thinks it is possible for this nation to go on spending more than it earns is possibly not smart enough to understand the deception when it bites them on the end of the nose. In fact, it often occurs to me that it is simply the work of the devil!"

By now, the old man was trembling, and he was rising from his chair as if answering a primal call, irresistible and edged with excitement. Robert Anderson feared he had pushed Peter P. Pence to the brink of endurance, that his heart might explode, and that he, Robert Anderson, Pulitzer prize-winning southern correspondent for the *New York Times,* might be held accountable for it. The onus was one he did not welcome.

Peter P. Pence stood in front of his antique rocking chair, straightened himself as much as he could, and then said, low and even and with unmistakable clarity as Pumpkin flinched, as she always did when the master pounded the black walnut cane against the wide, pegged planks beneath his feet:

"Now, I will ask you to go and leave me to tend my own fire. Should you return next Sunday, you should know that I will begin with the eleventh commandment: *Thou shalt not spend more than thou earneth.*"

A cold, sharp wind surged to meet Robert Anderson as he walked down the hill to his car. He looked up at the stars painted across the sky, as smooth as an inverted bowl with sparkling indicators of possibly hundreds, even thousands of other as yet undiscovered civilizations. Each might have its own complexities of religious diversity. Some civilizations might be only beginning, while others were possibly ending. Still others might be on the edge of remarkable discovery about themselves, while others might be engaged in civil wars, mighty armies clashing, bayonets steaming with human blood—blood of a brother drawn by a brother. Beyond each failure lay root causes: greed, insensitivity, individualism in a free fall, mass psychosis, megalomania. Perhaps in every case, neglect of the simple value of something as small and fundamental as the penny lay squarely at the heart of the trouble.

A shooting star arced the late November sky, and Robert Anderson thought, as he often did, how it would be on Planet Earth when its day of total destruction would come, when, in a flash, all of mankind would be sluiced together with rivers, oceans, forests, deserts, and arctic ice—all creatures falling from their places. As quickly as the thought would come, it would go again, leaving Anderson with, perhaps, a greater sense of Planet Earth's human inhabitants being forever in disagreement about economic, social and theological order, caught on either side or in the middle of civil war as barbaric and brutal as the one in Rwanda in 1994-1995, or as in Oklahoma City at two minutes past nine on the morning of April 19, 1995—Anderson remembered the picture of the dying child, cradled in the warmth of the fireman's arms.

Anderson also remembered Maria in 1982, the peasant woman in El Salvador, who had gone to town to sell her three loaves of bread, but was killed when she stumbled into the crossfire of the government and rebel soldiers. Maria's body was covered and her small, red purse lay empty in the dirt, but there was a cup on the sidewalk beside her. People were dropping centavos into the cup. It would help to pay for her flimsy, wooden coffin.

CHAPTER TWO

Grandfathers Jake and Daniel had grown up proud and stubborn in the dogtrot, two log cabins built end to end, separated by a connecting passageway big enough for dogs to trot and for humans to stack three nights' supply of firewood on either side. Born in 1839 and having lost their parents to the cholera epidemic of '49, the brothers had disagreed fundamentally on the issues of slavery and of a state's right to do as it damn well pleased. In 1860, they were a relatively old and gnarled 21 years of age, as guarded as two prehistoric groundhogs furiously suffering one another in a burrow with two entrances, tunnels set too close for comfort, without enough elbow room to accommodate petty peeves.

The brothers had taken childlike brides to live in the house divided, but the War had begun for certain, and the twins, looking exactly alike except for a birthmark on the inside of Daniel's right leg, had gone in opposite directions—Jacob to the north side of the Ohio River for the first time in his life, Daniel to the south side of the Kentucky River, the farthest he'd ever been or ever would be from home.

They'd hardly passed their respective first musters, had barely dressed in their darling blue and grey, had no more than affixed bayonets to their firing pieces, when their courses brushed like stars burning in the Milky Way above a little town, a name they'd not heard before. They'd come whisker-close to sinking into the muck of carnage at Perryville—bodies scattered in death alongside split-rail fences, so many vacant blue eyes staring blankly at the heavens, the brothers coming, at last, face to face in the drought-stricken hills along the Doctor's Fork of the blood-fed Chaplin River.

Oh, they'd fallen together all right, Jake and Daniel, searching each other's red and swollen eyes, seeing for the first time the awful truth of what they'd done to themselves.

Peter P. Pence's grandfathers had been like so many other divided families of the time, in what would be remembered as the Battle of Perryville, Kentucky, October 8, 1862, also called the Battle of Chaplin Hills, possibly the fiercest and bloodiest as any battle in the Civil War, when considering the briefness of the engagement. Jacob, the paternal grandfather, served with the 15th Kentucky Brigade in the Army of the Ohio under the command of Major General Don Carlos Buell. Peter's maternal grandfather, Daniel, also shed his blood upon the ground and came within a heartbeat of losing his life in Leonidas Polk's Confederate Right Wing in the Army of Mississippi under the command of General Braxton Bragg.

> *"Give it to 'em, boys, give 'em what General Cheatham says."*
> Confederate General and Episcopal Bishop Leonidas Polk
> *"Give 'em hell boys."*
> Confederate General Benjamin F. Cheatham

Jake and Daniel had sustained spiritual wounds too, sending them back home together, slowly, limping like two old, bedraggled, shame-faced, shitty-assed sheep, hooves curled and moldering, psychic wounds burning in a bottomless pit, mental scars making forgiveness and future relationships troublesome. To boot, they were penniless.

"Jake," said Daniel, "reckon this road home wide 'nough f'r the two of us?"

"Dan'l," said Jake, "hit damn well have to be, 'cause hit's the onliest one we got."

"Jake," said Daniel, "reckon we gonna have any money again? Reckon we ever gonna be good brothers, raise up children so as not to fight no more?"

"Dan'l," said Jake, with his left hand reaching inside his bloodstained shirt, pulling out a dirty, hardened biscuit, breaking it in two with the strength of one hand, giving half to his brother, "Dan'l, we been catawamptiously chawed up and spit out."

"Never should'a fit first place."

"Gawddam piece'a foolness."

"That'n then some," said Daniel, hobbling with a piece of locust limb, the fork of it as snug as it was possible to be inside his blistered right armpit, the improvised crutch taking the place of the leg now stinking in a heap of arms and legs in the sideyard of a Danville church. In Perryville, Jake's right arm lay amid another pile of amputated limbs, well on their way to rotting and sinking into the earth like fertilizer to enrich it.

> *"The guns were discharged so rapidly that it seemed the earth itself was in a volanic uproar. The iron storm passed through our ranks, mangling and tearing men to pieces. The very air seemed full of stifling smoke and fire which seemed the very pit of hell, peopled by contending demons."*
>
> Private Sam Watkins
> First Tennessee Volunteer Infantry
> Confederate States Army

> *"The dead lay just as they had fallen. Some with features calm and serene, others ghostly and distorted, some mangled and torn, others pierced by a single ball."*
>
> Lt. R.V. Marshall
> 22nd Indiana Volunteer Infantry
> U.S. Army

> *"I always shot at privates. It was they that did the shooting
> and killing, and if I could kill or wound a private, why my
> chances were so much the better. I always looked upon officers
> as harmless personages."*
>
> Private Sam Watkins
> First Tennessee Volunteer Infantry
> Confederate States Army

In Harrodsburg, at the Graham Springs Hotel, converted into a major hospital, the pile of amputated arms and legs reached to the ballroom balcony on the second floor.

"Jake," said Daniel, breathing hard with the throbbing pain of his stumped leg, "s'pose there'll be some child of one of us that'll live right, do right?"

"Doubt hit," said Jake, "For ever seed sown there's hunnerds, thousands, Gawd knows how many, come to nothin'. Only onct in a great while does a tree grow tall, bearin' dependable fruit, givin' reliable shade."

Jake had straggled in from the ghostly stinking hell of the battlefield, and after a week of searching, he'd found Daniel in the improvised hospital in the little church in nearby Danville. The surgeons had already removed Daniel's leg as methodically as the Union doctors had taken Jake's arm. After the supply of chloroform and morphine had played out, there had been the gulping of the rotgut whiskey, then the slicing and the sawing, as swift and clean as peeling apples and chopping firewood: the cutting of the skin, the laying it back, then the sawing, finally the tucking of the skin flaps and the sewing of it to hold as a basket for the bone. There'd been the stifled screams, the biting down on the bullet until it felt as if teeth would be pulled loose from moorings, the delirium, then the helpless, sagging feeling of desperate weightlessness, the morose, nightmarish sleep, the waking up—and the wanting—"Oh, my Gawddd"—the *wanting* to go home.

"Dear boy," said a volunteer nurse, "dear boy, you'll be going home, all right."

The brothers' once proud and shining blue and gray uniforms were forlornly shredded; by looking, two weeks after the amputations, it could not be told on which side they had fought. In general appearance they favored both sheep and groundhogs. Unlike sheep they were in no mind to give up, but like groundhogs they knew instinctively there was waiting for them a hole in the hollow of home if they'd be patient enough to hobble their way back to it.

On the first night, they camped quietly together with their tin cups of pilfered milk and their legs and wings of stolen chicken. Warming by a small fire, the brothers spoke hardly at all to any stranger, wanting only to be reunited away from the hideous, wrenching madness of the war. The warriors hitched a ride on a farmer's wagon as far as Pleasant Hill, where tireless Shakers fed thousands of soldiers at long tables set up in the yard on the east side of the Trustees' Office. The two brothers became inseparable, bonded with speech curtailed and mumbled, indicative of distrust of every other living creature, including the Shakers with their dour and troubled faces of doubted peace, their diminished hope for the future of the celibate sect.

The one overriding desire of Jake and Daniel was to find their way back home to their wives. Only 75 miles on a straight line, it would become a long, agonizingly slow and arduous journey, weaving the waterways, stumbling up and down steep and seldom-traveled ravines, finding pockets of fears and hostilities among a people beset by Morgan's Raiders and maurauding guerillas with allegiances to none but their vengeful selves.

Jake and Daniel bargained for passage on a flatbottom boat leaving from the Shakertown Landing, the primitive log craft inching upstream, leaving behind the October majesty of the Kentucky River Palisades. Jake was a grateful one-armed oarsman and Daniel was an alternate one-legged steersman, as they picked their way through the narrowing depths of the river in that drought year of '62.

When they reached the mouth of the Red River, more shallow still and snaggletoothed with fallen trees, Jake and Daniel set out on foot, heading eastward over the Warrior's Trail through Indian Fields, the wide valley that in the previous century had been the bloody killing fields for buffalo herds: onward toward the dogtrot in the Pocket.

Jacob and Daniel had come home to their birthplace, thankfully and hungrily to their young, eager, tearful but resolute wives—Suffiah and Armilda—youthful yet quickly aging women who smoked their pipes with shy and furtive glances from beneath their homemade, sun-faded bonnets. They were the long-suffering stalwarts who'd waited loyally, patiently and prayerfully in separate halves of the old log house with the connecting roofed passageway, the wives crossing back and forth many times over the dogtrot, sharing their worries, their hopes and the same fireplace in the winter of 1861.

"Suffie," said Armilda, "when our men comin' back?"

"Millie," said Suffiah, "after they git their asses whupped."

CHAPTER THREE

I need more time," said Robert Anderson on the telephone from his office in Atlanta to his editor in New York.

"How much, for Christ's sake?" said the editor.

"Maybe weeks. Yes, weeks."

"What the hell are you talking about? We need your piece finished in early December."

"Listen, Charlie." said Anderson, "You've got to trust me on this one. You've trusted me before, and I've never let you down. I don't intend to start now. I'll begin filing weekly summaries of where I am in the piece. All I ask is that you don't jump the gun. Stick with me. This will make you proud. Not only that, it may do some honest-to-God good at a time when the damned country *needs* it."

"Bob, Bob, Bob. O.K. O.K. O.K. Keep working. Keep working. Keep working. But I want to see those weekly reports."

"As long as you don't jump the gun with an early release, unless of course, something happens to me in the Pocket."

"What the hell does that mean?"

"Has nothing to do with my expense account, Charlie, although, I suppose it does, come to think of it."

"Robert Anderson, Pulitzer prize-winning Robert Anderson, don't give me any shit."

"Charlie, trust me. Can you trust me?"

"Just bring home the bacon."

"Don't worry. This one will make us all proud to be journalists."

"Bullshit."

The week sped by with Robert Anderson's mind racked by the stubborn refusal of the eleventh commandment to yield to compromise. He consulted authorities, financial experts, political scientists and economic technocrats. A professor of economics at Emory University in Atlanta, knowing first-hand the shallowness of Anderson's understanding of financial theories, allowed him to borrow Michael Parkin's textbook, *Economics*.

According to Parkin, the United States of America in a ten-year period *tripled* the national debt from $1 *trillion* to $3 *trillion*; the national government had blithely *spent* $100 billion more than it received in taxes every year from 1982 to 1992. Parkin, educated in England and, at the time of the publication of his book, on the faculty in the Department of Economics at the University of Western Ontario, Canada, had with apparent amusement, perhaps sadness, looked across the border and seen a pathetically "Spendthrift Uncle Sam."

Professor Parkin had posed an often asked question, "Does a government deficit impose a burden on future generations?" All of Robert Anderson's intuition screamed northward, high across the U.S.-Canadian border: "Yes, and if anybody doesn't think so, come with me on my weekly visits with Peter P. Pence. He knows it doesn't take anything more than common sense to figure out that a deficit is the negative difference between income and outgo, and accumulated deficit is *mounting* debt, which somebody, someday, is going to have to pay."

There were many tempting pretenses for stretching outgo beyond income, but for Anderson a central truth could not logically be tilted askew, much less turned on its head. It was indisputable. Spending more than an individual, company, or governmental entity EARNED was fundamentally fallacious, if not today, then tomorrow, if not tomorrow then the day after. One day *all* chickens *would* come home to roost, as Peter P. Pence liked to say. All civil war survivors would limp back to their Pockets.

Frederick Cartwright had spoken clearly about "war, pestilence and famine" in his book, *Disease and the World*, and it had stamped a stinging impression on the mind of Robert Anderson. Cartwright's "War is a psychotic disorder" could easily be correlated to Wordsworth's "getting and spending we lay waste our powers."

Deficit spending is, and always would be the spreading of what Peter P. Pence would most likely call a monstrous myth to individuals ready to fall for another "something for nothing" seduction. Meantime, the economic experts wandering through the thickets of their technocracies would continue to argue that individuals could never be trusted to develop and use their God-given intuitive intelligence.

On the second Sunday of meetings with the old man in the dogtrot, Robert Anderson again sat by the fireplace, where he acknowledged:

"Maybe you're right. Your eleventh commandment, *Thou shalt not spend more than thou maketh,* maketh absolute sense," he said with his warmest and sassiest smile, hopeful for pleasant cheer.

Peter P. smiled back at Robert Anderson.

"I thought perhaps you would come to this understanding."

"I'm not there yet, but you're doing a pretty good job of bringing me along. Frankly, I would never presume that you would reveal your secret to me, but I did feel that you might give me a few good ideas, parts, at least, of that secret," Anderson continued from his place on the nail keg before the fire.

"Young man, in all of creation there are no secrets. One who does not believe oneself in possession of such a 'secret' simply has not yet understood what is obvious."

"The solution to my problems lies right before my eyes?"

"Exactly."

"I need encouragement."

"I'll give you that, for I sense you are sincere and therefore honest."

"Thank you."

"I have made it a practice to acquire many books during my lifetime, very nearly 100 years now," said Peter as he drew a circle around the room wrapped by shelves of books reaching from the floor to the ceiling. "All of these books are my acquaintances, some I consider to be members of my family, a few are like the grandparents I never knew. One of my favorites is Booker T. Washington's *Up from Slavery*, and there is a favorite line in it that has meant as much to me as the First Amendment to the Constitution of the United States or John Milton's *Areopagitica*."

Robert Anderson leaned forward on the nail keg and hung on the words coming from Peter P. Pence.

"Put your bucket down where you are," he continued.

"What does that mean to you?" Anderson asked.

"Booker T. Washington intended for it to mean, when you are in touch with your true self, you are nearest the resolution of all your problems. Many theologians will dismiss this as deism, economists will call it naive, but I find myself quite in tune with Whitman's "Song of Myself" and Benjamin Franklin's *Poor Richard's Almanac*. I have another book here, which both amuses and instructs. It is Lawrence Peter's *The Peter Principle*. He cites 'Finster's Law of Location.'"

"'Finster's Law of...'?"

"Location—'Finster's Law of Location'—wherever you go, there you are."

"Another way of saying, you're saddled with your *self*, cannot escape your *self*, and therefore it makes imminent sense to be at peace with your *self* and make the most of the potential of *yourself*," Anderson pleased himself in abstracting.

"You have it. Do you see these ten kernels of corn?"

"From your garden?"

"Yes. Now let us say that these ten kernels of corn are all I have. Yet, I need to pay for something costing 11 kernels of corn. I am one kernel short. Where is that extra kernel of corn?"

"It is not among the ten?"

"Nay, nor is it among the *nine*, for I have already set aside one kernel for my principal, a portion of the secret that I'll reveal to you at our next meeting."

"Well, if the kernel of corn you need is not among the ten, not even among nine of the ten, the kernel of corn you need is—is yet to be grown in your garden!?"

"Now you understand the mystery of the units of work, which of course is only a troubling, onerous mystery to those who fail to see the obvious, or they see it, don't like the sight of it and reject it. My *need* will simply have to wait until the next crop of corn is in the crib, and the only way for that to happen is for me to be about the business of the growing of my and my Father's corn in the proper season."

"But, the creditor may *demand* the one kernel of corn before it's time to plant."

"That is true. But that is far less likely to happen if there is an understanding between the creditor and the debtor, built over time, so that the creditor knows that there are special situations when it is in his best interest..."

"To *earn* interest."

"Yes, because the earning of interest is legitimate. It only becomes unethical when it becomes usurious. This is precisely what caused my brother Adam's downfall. He believed the ocean was no deeper than his capacity for loan sharking. He lived by it and his mouth was filled with sand by it."

"Legitimate interest, then, is much the same as growing a crop of corn."

"Certainly. And I have always been willing to pay legitimate interest, as I have been to grow legitimate corn, but I have never lost sight of the need to be growing a better crop of corn, saving the first kernel out of each ten, while depending on lenders to be charging ethical rates of interest while they save 10% of all *they* earn."

"Everyone should be doing this?"

"Absolutely."

"Even governments?"

"As surely as tying shoestrings. There must be a new effort, a new product, a new service, something with new value for which a new reward is obtained. *The New York Times* must put out a newspaper every day. What goes into it should be as true as possible, as unbiased as possible, as fair as possible."

"All the news that's fit to print," smiled Anderson.

"The work is in the horse, the corn is in the cart..."

"On the way to the crib..."

"On the way to some animal's stomach..."

"On the way to someone's table..."

"With a fair payment coming back..."

"To the principal..."

"With 10% set aside at both ends of the deal, ah, yes, you are very quick, young man, and I like our conversations, truly I do."

"I wouldn't trade them for anything."

"So, you will remember: the eleventh commandment: *Thou shalt not spend more than thou earneth*. The only way to get around a mathematical difference is to borrow the needed number, and in the equation of the kernels of corn you will need to borrow 12, not 11."

"I'm lost."

"I know. It's because you journalists are seldom familiar with the Ten Commandments, so I wouldn't expect you to know about the thirteenth. But, before we talk about that two weeks from now, we must discuss the twelfth commandment, and we will do that next Sunday. You will return?"

"Yes."

"Good. Now I must rest. I grow tired much more quickly from talking than I used to. My heart, you see, has pounded so many times inside this old chest in the past century there must inevitably come the time when it will have no choice but to cease."

"I understand."

"You are welcome to stay while I rest. Perhaps you will want to read more from my journal of 1918, or perhaps you will re-discover and consider the differences of a Richard Harding Davis and an Ambrose Bierce."

"Beauty and the Beast?" mused Robert Anderson. "Mr. Pence, you never cease to amaze me. Here you are, living in a dogtrot in Kentucky, surrounded by books, telling a *New York Times* correspondent he ought to be reading his Richard Harding Davis and his Ambrose Bierce."

"Why should that surprise you?"

"Because it is so unusual. I would expect hardly anybody in suburban Atlanta or hideaways in Connecticut to have read Davis or Bierce, certainly not to have them as accessible as—"

"Turning on a television set?"

"Yes."

"That is because, young man, your generation has become largely a generation of non-readers. There are many exceptions, of course, and there are increasing numbers of publishing industry customers, but the largest herd is internetting in their cyberspaces."

"Mr. Pence, are you going to tell me that you've been surfing?"

"I certainly am not. My cyberspace is within my own brain, and my internetting is with God. But, who knows, if I had another 100 years to live, I might consider chattering with other brains, unseen through computers and satellites, living on other planets, although I rather doubt it."

"You said you wanted to rest," said Anderson kindly.

"Yes I did. And I will. Make yourself at home with Davis and Bierce, or any of my other friends."

Robert Anderson spent the rest of the day leafing through the books on the shelves of Peter P. Pence's dogtrot library, reliving through *The*

Media in America, a History, Adolph Ochs' purchase, in 1896, of the *New York Times* at auction for only $75,000. The August 19, 1896, issue had described Ochs' intent: "...to make the columns of the *Times* a forum for the consideration of all questions of public importance."

Anderson relished the simple clarity and vigor of Richard Harding Davis' accounts of the events leading up to the official American entry into World War I, April 6, 1917. The popular former correspondent for the *New York Journal* and the *New York Sun* and editor of *Harper's Weekly* seemed at the time of his death in 1916 to have greatly matured since his "rough riding days" with Teddy Roosevelt in the Spanish-American War.

By 1914, Ambrose Bierce had disappeared in Mexico, but his *Devil's Dictionary* with all its feisty, irreverent cynicism was alive and well in 1999, and his "An Occurrence at Owl Creek Bridge" had not lost its vivid, descriptive energy. Bierce would live on as the classic iconoclast, the breaker of bubbles, the fiercely independent writer who would give the First Amendment its richness, its truest and most challenging, yet cherished reason for being. He would also be forever remembered as the idiot to have had no more sense than to write so crudely about the assassination of Kentucky Governor William Goebels, wildly calling for the assassination of President William McKinley. It would remain a huge stain on the memories of both Bierce and his publisher, William Randolph Hearst, and it went to the heart of yellow journalism.

The recalling of some of the giants of journalism—Bierce, Davis, Ochs, Pulitzer and Hearst—on a Sunday afternoon in a remote pocket of Kentucky, was a gentle, nudging reminder to Robert Anderson that the day of his own reflective time of life in retirement was dawning—that he'd always have Peter P. Pence to thank for it.

Anderson turned to look at Peter, who had stretched out upon his pallet, Pumpkin nuzzled at his side, and the reporter wondered, no, marvelled at the old man's self-containment, his apparent self-contentment. "If only I," whispered Robert Anderson to himself, "if only

I had the courage and the wisdom to live the life of a Peter P. Pence, what a fine thing that would be."

Anderson rubbed his eyes, cleaned his glasses and quietly left the dogtrot, for it was necessary to return to his motel room 30 miles away to write the next installment of his story for Mr. Adolph Ochs' newspaper. Anderson would remember to be as clear and clean in his writing as Richard Harding Davis, as irreverent as Ambrose Bierce and as "accurate, accurate, accurate" as Joseph Pulitzer. Anderson, whose reputation had been built on his ability to burrow deeply into the lives of his news sources, returned again and again to the files of the local newspaper, as well as to the personal journals of Peter P. Pence.

CHAPTER FOUR

The brothers, Jacob and Daniel, had returned home in tolerable peace in 1862 to rebuild the farm left to them by their mother and father, Leondas and Jessie, the children of Chad and Annabelle and Jeremiah and Lucy Ann, the earliest progenitors who'd floated down the Ohio in the late 18th century to stake their claim in the Pocket.

After Perryville, Jacob and Daniel at once became too busy with their individual and collective lives to argue any more about whatever it was that had sent them off to fight over it in a Civil War. Their minds and their bodies had been numbed by the screaming hell of the Chaplin Hills, and to each half of the reunited log house a child would be born— Patience in Jake and Suffiah's side, Prudence in Daniel and Armilda's. Like a reprieve from conflict, the new war babies had become like the brightest stars on clear nights of the autumn moon, like the one on October 8, 1862, in the rolling valley of the Chaplin River, when the madness finally ended and the buzzards the next day began to circle where more than 1,000 lay dead, and more than 5,000 were stumbling away with wounds of every sort.

In less than two decades, with the passage of a new generation in the Pocket, Patience and Prudence Pence, the living children of the war that had killed 600,000 people, were growing up with old scars slowly beginning to heal. Yet, dear prices for such a costly, stupid civil war were yet to be compensated, and there were those who believed that tolls would be exacted as surely as wages of sin after a fall.

Patience and Prudence, like two peas in a pod, as much like brother and sister as they were first cousins, played together, simultaneously discovered their bodies and the commonality of the sweetness of life together. They became as inseparable as their fathers. They married in 1879, when they were 16 years old, the sap rising in the young lovers with the swiftness of a spring season along the creek at the foot of the hill.

The onslaught of cholera in 1876 had taken away Jacob, Suffiah, Daniel and Armilda, their deaths leaving Patience and Prudence more dependent on one another than they ever imagined possible. They christened their first child, Paul, their second, a girl, Paula, the proud, new patriarchs putting much stock in the life of the Apostle Paul, always a favorite of Armilda's, who'd learned to read while Daniel had been off fighting for the Confederacy. She had taught Prudence to read, and she in turn had taught her husband, Patience, and together each night by candlelight they had pored over favored passages in their Bible. They could understand and love words as simple, as sure and as clear as: "For in him we live, and move, and have our being...." It was a sweet, clean, youthful thought as gentle as the breezes blowing across the dogtrot, making summers bearable.

The third child was also a girl, and they named her Angel, because Patience and Prudence believed God probably had sent her to bring hope to lives everywhere, as well as their own, especially after Paul's horrifying death, his little body so blackened by cholera that he had to be buried within minutes of his death. Next had come the boy, Adam, for whom Patience and Prudence had had the greatest of expectations. He would be the redeemer for the loss of Paul, he would restore order in the chaos swirling through the Pocket. But the stillborn triplets followed, the fifth, sixth and seventh children, all girls—Pansy, Petunia and Poppy— named by Prudence in a horrible frenzy, her body and spirit broken again by pain and humiliation. She named the miniature still lifes, named them for flowers in her garden, the three little girls becoming her morning

glory fantasies, her afternoon and evening esctasies.

Prudence, the quickly aging woman-child, spent hours in the garden, digging, praying, talking and arguing with herself, viciously weeding, then as sweetly as she knew she must, snugging the warm earth around the blossoming flowers. She could no more leave this spot on earth than she could forsake her very self, her very self, she said aloud, over and over. She was like one who knowingly lives on a flood plain, never dreaming nor daring to leave it no matter how many times the old Licking River rose and spewed and swept man and beast before it, swept them away as if they were no more than splintered pieces of wood. Approximately two years had separated the births of the ten babies of Prudence and Patience Pence—1880, 1882, 1884, 1886, 1888, 1890, then the fallow decade to 1900—each date duly recorded in the massive family "Parallel Bible" with its fine, illustrative engravings on steel and wood, and in colors, and "Awarded the First Premium for elegantly-bound and illustrated Family Bibles at the United States Centennial Exposition, September 27, 1876." Three years later, Patience, proudly and with grave determination, had inscribed a copy of the Bible as a wedding gift to his sweetheart: "Presented to Prudence Pence by her husband Patience Pence," the names appearing with painstakingly awkward penmanship, centered among the red and gold on the frontispiece framed by intricate and delicate designs suggesting infinity.

After Peter was born on New Year's Day at the turn of the century, the pages for births were full and the funeral bouquets for Armilda and Suffiah had become faded, crinkled bookmarks for "The Temple of Solomon" and "The Ascent of Elijah" in the Parallel Bible. Each bouquet had a small white bow at the base of the stems, the only reminders of the women who'd worked as hard as any men anywhere in the Pocket.

The only Pence child buried up on the hill behind the log house, along with Jake and Suffiah and Daniel and Armilda had been Paul, the picture of health at the age of three when, in 1883, he had been stricken with the dreaded cholera. The first daughter, Paula, was one year old at the time, and the second daughter, Angie, was no more than the look that came to Patience's eyes once every year, or so it seemed, when he was the freest to be rip-roaring with Prudence under the kivvers at night, 'goin' the whole hog' as he liked to say with a slight smile streaked on his sun-baked face, while on Prudence's forehead and tightening mouth there widened a contortion with furrowing wrinkles of fearful disgust, the vague but numbing rememberance of pain and shame.

Cholera had plagued many parts of the nation in '32, '49, '66 and '73, and from time to time with no warning at all it had sprung up in places like the Pocket and too many preachers had always buzzed around it like hungry bees.

"Now—HUH—brothers and sisters—HUH—what you have here is nothin' more, and nothin' less—HUH—than God—HUH—a-thundren' his truth about SIN—HUH. What you have here is nothin' more, and nothin' less—HUH—than God—HUH—a-speakin' to you—HUH—a-punishin' you—HUH—and as long as you—HUH—keep a-sinnin'—HUH—He gonna—HUH—come down hard on you—HUH—wicked, good for nothin'—HUH—SCUM of the earth—HUH!"

Patience had heard the last sermon he ever would hear in the Rock Ledge Church, and on a warm night in June he had appointed himself a committee of one to go and speak with Brother Bob. Patience called out to the Man of God, where he was sleeping with one of the widder women over on the fork running through 'Hell's Half Acre.'

"Brother Bob, you come out cheer."

Brother Bob's head appeared in one of the upstairs windows, and he shouted back, "Now see here, Patience Pence, you've no right to be a-callin' me from my bed in the middle of the night. You've no right to be takin' out on me the death of your first born. You've no right to blame me for the deaths of any of your gol-damn fam'ly. You've no right to sass back at Gawd—HUH—when all's he's a-doin' is a-sendin' you a liddle bit more of the chol'ra as a minder that you are a SINNER, Patience Pence, a SINNER, you and your wife, Prudence, are SINNERS and don' you—HUH—fergit it neither—HUH!"

Patience's Colt .45 spoke back to Brother Bob and at the same time cleaned out all the panes in the window above his head. The explosion echoed through 'Hell's Half Acre': POW...POW...Pow...Pow...pow... pow...pow—the last pow fading into the fog settling in like a light comforter likely would on a coolish night, but the next words sharp and clear and leaving no doubt as to purpose:

"Brother Bob, you git your ass down here, and you git it down here NOW."

In less than a minute, Brother Bob was at the front door. He was slavering at the mouth and trembling from head to foot, like a dog that knows he's about to be goodly whipped. He held his hands behind his head and locked them there. He was sputtering terribly: "Mmis, Mmis, P-P-Pence, whoa, whoa, whoa, d-d-donn', d-d-onn', shoooot, shoooot, oh, oh, oh, sweeeet JESUSSSSS, d-d-donn' shoooot me."

"Lemmie me tell you something, Brother Bob, you hain't worth shootin', and I hain't *gonna* shoot you lessen I absolutely have to, 'cause then I'd be bound to dig the grave and put you IN it, and I hain't got time to do that, 'cause I've got my wife, Prudence, to care for now that we done put our first born into the ground, so what I'm a-tellin you, Brother Bob, is that you git your sweet ass down this road and out this Pocket and if'n I ever *see* you in here again, I will squarely put one of these .45 slugs 'tween your damned *eyes*."

As Brother Bob cleared the split rail fence at the widder woman's front yard, Patience raised the Colt .45 and laid a shot about an inch above Brother Bob's tousled head of hair, and it was never remembered that Brother Bob ever once returned to the Pocket. Other preachers would come and go, and some of them would be several cuts above Brother Bob, but the entire idea of cholera being a weapon in the arsenal of "God's wrath" as a punishment for general sins committed was more than Patience's instinctive beliefs could accommodate, more than right-minded men of God could lay upon the heads and hearts of a God-fearing people.

"Aw, sheet," muttered Patience, who generally said these two favorite damning words whenever he believed devilment needed a serious dressing down. His father, Jake, had grumbled "Aw, sheet" many times at the Battle of Perryville where all those good men on both sides were killed or wounded, scattered like firewood, faces hideously torn by explosives.

While the widder woman pulled the kivvers up over her head, Patience went home to see to the suffering of Prudence after the burying of their son, and Patience and Prudence were never again seen or heard of in the Rock Ledge Church.

They knew they hadn't sinned, at least not so much that God would take his anger out on them by sending the cholera in the middle of the night to have it strike their first born son. No God would make a child suffer so that he would scream and retch and have the scours like a common calf in the field. No God, at least no good God, would torment a teenage mother who had never done any wrong to anybody, a quiet young woman who had learned from her mother and father and from their mothers and fathers before them that it *was* a sin to do certain bad things in life—that it was sinful to be filled constantly with lust, or hate, or unforgivingness, or selfishness, or deliberately to cause pain and suffering in others, whether it be to humans, including oneself, or to the good earth itself. Yes, certain bad things would be considered sinful and, certainly, "Vengeance is mine" sayeth the Lord, and yet, God's forgiveness still might be possible if not likely, and a good God simply would not wreak retaliation in such a horrible way as to send cholera into the bodies of little children. Would He?

"Patience," said Prudence after they turned to walk away from the burying of Paul, "you s'pose the chol'ra come, you s'pose the chol'ra come 'cause of the wadder, 'cause of the wadder in the springhouse?"

"Could be," said Patience.

"I saw the fattenin' pigs 'round it." sighed Prudence. "I saw the derned fattenin' pigs 'round it and I *knew* I should'a said sumpin', I just knew I should'a said sumpin'," she moaned.

"I'll kill them pigs, kill ever damn last one of 'em," said Patience.

"You'll shoot them pigs and leave 'em to rot where they fall, leave 'em to rot where they fall, leave 'em to rot where they fall—but what will we do f'r wadder, f'r wadder, Patience?"

"Bring hit up from the f'r spring. Bile hit," said Patience as they neared the front steps of the log house.

"Patience, we hain't sinned, have we? Have we?"

"No, Prudence, we hain't sinned," answered Patience.

In the late 19th century, Prudence had become a totally worn-out woman, as catawamptiously chawed as Jake and Daniel had been at Perryville, and when the eighth and ninth children arrived, twin boys, Tommy "Poplar" and Bobby "Pine," she came the closest to losing the last ounce of her sanity. Patience, on the other hand, delighted in the strong and healthy sons and nothing would do but give them nicknames for his favorite trees. In the beginning the "liddle hilltoppers," as he proudly called them, were grounds for laughter, fun and frolicking times, filling Patience with foot-patting pride born of manliness on the nights of the full moon, but the twins were more than Prudence could bear, and by the time they were five years old, Poplar and Pine were royal hellions.

Finally, much later, there had appeared the tenth child—Peter—the "surprise," the "stranger who'd come to the door," the "angel boy that had come down from the sky," the afterthought, the never-expected, the impossibility, hardly a pebble much less a rock upon which to build any new generations in any new century. Subsequently, Peter had assigned himself the middle initial "P" to honor his frustrated, bone-tired parents.

By 1895, Patience and Prudence's brood had become hardly more than a scattered cluster of bad seed, a genetic bad dream exorcised only after the last drop of badness had been spilled, as disgusting as it was embarrassing. The two sweethearts had wanted nothing more than to love and to breathe life into new generations, had wanted to breathe the words of the Apostle Paul: "For in him we live, and move, and have our being."

By 1900, Paula was 18 and had run away to be married the first time. Angel was 16, her single-purposed mind filled with visions of midwifery and other exciting adventures described regularly in such dog-eared castaways as *Godey's Illustrated Magazine*, the *New York Sun*, and the *New York Times*, copies of the penny press filtering westward like winged water maple seeds.

Adam was 14, his hands eager to be tinkering with horseless carriages in town, equally talented as a petty thief, flattering, cajoling, specializing as a dandy, dowdy endearment to older women with silverware in their dining rooms and expensive costume jewelry in their bedrooms.

The triplets would have been 12 years old, but by the end of the first frenzied decade of the 20th century, they'd been fully reclaimed by the soil of the Pocket. They'd not experienced any far-flung metropolitan cities, where vivacious young women set their ribboned, feathered bonnets for older creatures caught in the whirlpool of top hats, bowlers, starched high collars, spats and gleaming patent leather shoes.

The twins were 10 years old, wild as March hares from the start. They'd go off hunting for days at a time, living like animals beneath the rock cliffs, falling in with moonshiners from whom, for "Poplar" at least, there was no turning back from disaster. He never left the Pocket alive. "Pine" saw the storm of alcoholism coming, and he had warned his brother, whom he dearly loved.

"You just have to stop it," said Pine.

"Hain't gonna stop nothin'," said Poplar.

"Hit gonna kill you," said Pine.

"Die happy," said Poplar, taking another long swig from the quart-sized demijohn.

The long summers and lonely winters of drinking moonshine had poisoned Poplar, despite all of Pine's warnings. They had worked together as lookouts at a still as hidden as it's possible to be in the hills of the Pocket, but the revenooers had found the boys there on that dark, moonless night and had carted them off to jail—and there was nothing that could have been said for it that would have made a particle bit of difference. The twins had become a mutually nurtured holy terror to themselves as well as their parents. Throwing away the key on the two little miserable "sheets," as Patience finally came to call them, would have been too good for them. After serving time they were released, Poplar immediately returning to being a lookout for a still, there to die one year later in a shoot-out with government agents. Pine had not gone back to the rock cliffs. The time in jail had cured him for certain.

"Hain't goin' back, Pop," Pine had said to Poplar.

"Where then?"

"Gonna be a doctor."

"Doctor a-what?"

"Gonna study in schools mainly about what happen to you and what could'a happen to me, Pop."

"Sheet. What you figger happen to me?"

"You're sick."

"Sheet. And you hain't?"

"No, I hain't, not yet I hain't, but I figger I could be, but even if I'm not sick, hit don't make me no bedder'n anybody."

"So where's this big-ass school you a-goin to?"

"First, gonna finish school here in the Pocket. Then I'm goin' to a university somers. Then I'm goin' to whichever medical place'll have me."

"With whose money?"

"I'll find a way. I'll work jobs. I'll git me one a-them scholarships. I'll count my pennies, Pop."

CHAPTER FIVE

Peter P. Pence was 18 years old when he volunteered to fight as a foot soldier in World War I. Serving with the U.S. 7th Infantry, Peter survived the battle of Chateau Thierry, where he acquitted himself in hand-to-hand combat against the German advance. He hated it, loathed the thrust of the bayonet into the chest of an 18-year-old German youth—*Thou shalt not kill*—hearing the sucking sound and the gasping for breath upon the pulling back of the glistening, cold steel, but at the same time unable not to be thrilled by it any less than Grandfathers Jacob and Daniel had been spurred on and on and on by the same thundering, gut-wrenching sounds of death at Perryville.

Peter had volunteered, same as his grandfathers, because he thought it was his solemn duty, no less than Jake and Dan'l had believed it theirs. They had all volunteered because they believed they were defending their land, their homes, their ideals.

"Did we do right by skedaddlin' after Perryville?"

"We weren't goin' any ferther north and we weren't goin' any ferther south. You lost a laig. I lost a arm. We could'a both stayed put and busted ourselves wide open, lost both arms and both laigs and let our guts run out and hit wouldn'a made no damn difference."

It was after the fighting was over in the "War to End all Wars" that the futility and the deep feeling of despair settled upon Peter, as it had upon his grandfathers. Why would humans continue such madness? Was it not a matter of economic power in both the American Civil War and the First World War? Would it not be ever so? Would it not lead to World War II and World War III? Yes, that is what it was. It was raw, economic power-madness, bereft of individual responsibility for the whole as well as the broken segments of the entirety. The American Civil War had killed 600,000, but World War I had cost the lives of more than ten *million* people, more than half of them civilians.

Peter P. Pence had fought with himself as much as he had the enemy at the Marne. A part of him had wanted to be pacifist, had wanted to hide in the Pocket and fight only when armies threatened the very 100-acre farm given to him by Patience and Prudence. He knew of many who had hidden from the draft just as his brothers, Poplar and Pine, had sought to evade the revenuers. Peter knew he could hide himself beneath the rock castles until Hell froze over, but there was another part of him that told him he had a responsibility to stand up for his United States, the nation reborn after Perryville, Shiloh, Chickamauga, Vicksburg, Chancellorsville and Gettysburg.

After the Armistice on the 11th hour of the 11th day of the 11th month in 1918, Peter had returned to the Pocket in Kentucky. He had supported the concept of the League of Nations, for he believed as President Wilson would insist—that the time had come for a new attempt at unity in the new, 20th century. Peter grieved for President Wilson as he sought valiantly, but in vain, to win U.S. Senate ratification of the Treaty of Versailles. The heartache would compound until the morning of February 3, 1924, when Woodrow Wilson, the 28th President of the United States, would die in his sleep, almost two months to the day before Adolph Hitler would be sentenced to jail for the beer hall putsch, as if a decent man would be buried in order for a despotic man to rise.

It was the "New Era of Prosperity" mounting toward the great Bull Market Boom of the late 1920s, the "Roaring Twenties" almost everywhere except in places like the log dogtrot in the Pocket in Kentucky, where Peter P. Pence had returned and lived quietly and as well as he always knew he would. Each issue of the *New York Times* usually arrived about one week late, which Peter liked because it discouraged quickness leading to rash and silly determinations. He had decided to subscribe to the *Times* after buying the November 11, 1918, issue at Grand Central Station in New York City after his return from Europe to begin the long train ride back to Cincinnati and from there on south to the Pocket in Kentucky.

As the new decade of decadence dawned, Peter watched with fascination as the stock market roared its approval of the election of Calvin Coolidge, churning more than 2,000,000 shares of stock to set new records on Wall Street. Two years later, many of the same issues, including the rails, "left the track" as experts tried to figure out what was happening.

Peter knew.

It was greed.

It was stupidity.

It was Perryville.

It was an abandonment of the simple arithmetic he'd learned from his first teacher, Bessie Cooper.

It was "Black Thursday," October 24, 1929.

"Buddy, can you spare a dime?"

In quieting winter seasons in the Pocket in Kentucky, during the early, desperate 1930s when strangers would suddenly appear at the front steps to the dogtrot, the requests were usually the same:

"Do you have work?"

"Do you have any milk?"

"Any bread?"

"Any eggs?"

"A piece of meat? Any kind of meat?"

"Can a man and his family sleep in the barn?"

Peter P. would always remember the last Christmas with his mother and father in 1910, and later he would recall each word of the conversation that had followed.

"Peter," said his father, "Ma and me don' have much longer on this here earth. We've heard the Lord finally a-callin'. He has spoke directly to us through His token. I saw the burnin' bush. Lightnin' likely done hit, but hit was the Lord God's lightnin' all right, I reckon.

"'You believe in the Lord?' were the very words of God Almighty.

"'I do,' I told 'im.

"'Well, if'n you do believe in the Lord, and if'n he wants you to come home tonight at midnight, you hain't gonna say no, are you?' he said in that bush that kept a-burnin'. Hit were the last thing he said.

"'Can't say no,' I told 'im, so naturally we're obliged to be a-goin' Home to take up our places with Him and them's that gone a'fore," Patience continued to explain to Peter. "You 'n Angie 'n Pine are our onliest hope. Since all our children, ceptin' you, are scattered to the ends of the earth, we are a-givin' you all the plunder you'll likely need.

"This 100 acres'll be yours, and this homeplace'll be yours. The corncrib'll be yours too...My pappy's 16-shot rifle'll be yours."

"And my pappy's Springfield'll be yours, be yours," smiled Prudence for the first time in a long time, "'cause if Patience goin' Home, I'll not be fer-a'hind-im, not be very fer-a'hind-im. The family Bible'll be yours of course, Peter," she added. "S'pose my sewin' basket and my spinnin' wheel'll be yours too, so as f'r you to be able to give 'em to your wife, when you do marry, when you do marry, 'cause Angie too busy a-midwifin' to be spendin' no time at no spinnin' wheels...no time at no spinnin' wheels."

"But I'm only ten years old," said Peter.

"Don't madder," said Patience. "Hain't time to waste. I saw the burnin' bush. Hain't time to wait on no Poplar to come home from no university. Hain't time to wait on no Angie to come home from no midwifin'."

"Peter, you're the one who's here, you're the one who's here, you're the one...."

"Everthing, lock, stock and barrel'll be yours, Peter, and you'll decide what to divvy up with Poplar and Angie," said Patience, worn out from talking. "But there's one other liddle thing. While back, I'd moseyed over to town, and I'd talked with some of Pap's buddies at the courthouse. See, there's this yankee feller passin' through and he was havin' a 'niption fit. Wanted to find some buyers for some papers he was in a lather to sell. Said he was repsentin' some rich folks up in Cincinnati and over in Louisville. Some mighty fretful folks, the way he went on about it, and he made me a rock-bottom offer and I said, aw sheet, I might's well part with some of the money your ma and me set by. So here, Peter, are the 'tificates for 100 shares of Union Pacific, 100 shares of 'Malgamated Copper and 100 shares of Standard Oil."

Patience handed the three pieces of paper to Peter and the little boy took them into his hands and stared at them. Never before in his life had he seen a stock certificate, but he knew instinctively that there must be value alone in the texture and the design of the paper. "Where shall I keep them?" he asked, looking into the hardened, wearied, deathly face of his father.

"You must find a hidin' place. There's a new bank in town, but I'm not right convinced hit's the safest place to keep nuthin'," said Patience.

"Pa," said Prudence, "if'n Peter keeps the 'tificates here in the house, the house might burn, the house might *burn*."

"True," replied Patience.

"If Peter carries the 'tificates with him, he might *lose* 'em, he might lose 'em," she added.

"True," said Patience.

"Body might just steal 'em from him, *steal* 'em....."

"True."

"If Peter hides 'em in a tool box and buries 'em here on the farm, he might fergit where he dug, or sumpin' might happen to him and no one'd know about the hidin' place, the *hidin'* place."

"True."

"Well?" said Prudence. "*Well?*"

Patience had gone empty on words.

"I have an idea." said Peter, "If you want me to take responsibility for these things, and I'm mighty proud and grateful that you do, why not let me keep them for right now under my pillow? Later I'll decide a better place. I promise to be fair to Angie and Pine, and I promise to be careful."

If Peter was anything, he was careful. He'd been the first in the family to attend school either seriously or regularly, and he'd been one of the reasons why Pine had decided to patch together enough credits to sweet talk his way to graduation from high school. For Peter, it had begun when he started reading books suggested to him by the young woman who'd come down from Cincinnati to begin her life's work, she said, teaching yesterday's people to try to do a better job about being tomorrow's people, not just today's people. When he was 65 years old, Peter would read Jack E. Weller's *Yesterday's People,* and he would understand it and appreciate it, and he'd think back to when he was five years old, and Bessie Cooper had given Peter a copy of *McGuffey's Third Eclectic Reader*, and together they had feasted on it better than watermelon at a church revival. Peter was also fascinated by John J. Anderson's 1872 *A Manual of General History, Being an Outline History of the World from the Creation to the Present Time.*

"Peter," Bessie would say, "I want you to learn to speak more correctly, not because it makes you better than your parents, but because it's a good idea to improve in all ways possible. Speech is just one way."

"Miz Bessie," Peter had said in the beginning, "I wont to tawk like you."

"And you will, Peter," Bessie had said, and she'd drilled him with McGuffey's articulation exercises. She became so obsessed with teaching Peter P. Pence that she visited daily in the old log dogtrot. While Prudence labored with flax at her spinning wheel, the look of despair darkening in her downcast eyes, the soft murmuring repetitiousness of words forever connected to the triplets, woven as tenaciously as kudzu vines, the dusky hair parted severely in the middle and pulled back hard against the top edge of her ears, Patience coming in with another armload of firewood, Bessie and Peter would work at the big table in the center of the room. Patience and Prudence seemed to know instinctively not to interfere, neither out of pride nor of pigheadedness, of which they had inherited plenty.

Bessie wore a white pinafore with a huge bow, with white-laced cuffs resting comfortably on her wrists as her fingers helped hold the paper where Peter practiced his longhand assignments. Bessie knew through her own intuition that the little boy was a tomorrow person trapped in today's circumstances, shaped in so many ways by the yesterdays of Prudence and Patience and Jacob and Daniel and Suffiah and Armilda and Chad and Annabelle and Jeremiah and Lucy Ann before them.

Peter was a sweet man-child. Early on, he had developed an uncommon confidence in his ability to make decisions on his own say. As unfortunate as seven of his brothers and sisters had been, Peter shone like a fine, newly minted coin. He kept the stock certificates beneath the pillow still stuffed with straw, because he never liked the softness of chicken feathers. Each night, before falling asleep, Peter would recite a prayer he'd memorized from the McGuffey Reader, Bernard Barton's "An Evening Prayer":

> *Before I close my eyes in sleep,*
> *Lord, hear my evening prayer,*
> *And deign a helpless child to keep,*
> *With thy protecting care.*

> *Thus mayst thou guard with gracious arm*
> *The bed whereon I lie,*
> *And keep a child from every harm*
> *By thine own watchful eye.*

Then Peter would feel beneath the pillow and with his right hand he'd again smooth the certificates. He respected his mother and father for having entrusted them to him, and he knew he must find a better place to keep them. Fire was a constant threat, and he did not wish to gamble on the constant possibility of an out-of-control chimney fire. Theft was also a risk, and he did not wish to build his new life by taking pointless, unthoughtout chances. In that regard, he had a healthy fear of his brother, Adam, who was always out there somewhere, running with the coyotes, and worst of all, the coydogs.

"This Sunday, I should like to discuss with you the twelfth commandment for I believe you are ready for the abundance of it."

"Tell me," said Robert Anderson on the third Sunday of his visits with Peter P. Pence.

"Thou shalt save the FIRST ten cents of each $1.00 that passeth through thy hands."

"It sounds familiar," Robert Anderson acknowledged.

"There are many, I suppose, who make a big thing out of tithing for their churches, and by that they seem to have been convinced that it unquestionably means that they are giving back 10% of their gross checks directly to God."

"God and churches are not the same thing?"

"Many times. There are worthy exceptions, but taken on the whole, churches are unfortunately made up of tricky human beings. Some church officials blatantly steal from bank accounts as well as Sunday collection plates."

"God and human beings—not the same thing?"

"I think you're understanding it. In Ralph Waldo Emerson's essay, 'Self-Reliance,' there is the uniquely American notion that individuals do not need representatives at Judgment Day nearly so much as they need *themselves*, and *themselves* in good order, in good standing. Well, if that is true at Judgment Day, and I believe it is, why is it not every bit as

true *every moment* of one's life?"

"Everyone is not so well disciplined and principled and Emersonian as you."

"Most of the population has been conditioned to think in a non-Emersonian way, a non-Henry David Thoreau, a non-Walt Whitman way. Beginning at the age of five when we all were geniuses, should the truth be known, authorities within and without the churches begin to hammer us with 'Original Sin,' and the preposterous idea that we don't know what's good for ourselves. Too often church leadership loses touch with everyday people. So, we are taxed, saddled with guilt and sold a bill of goods, which is supposed to improve our chances of arriving in Heaven with all our papers in order. Outrageous deception."

"The tithe, then, is the church's *tax*?"

"Of course. You understand, tithing is also a central part of my 'secret' as you call it, but what I have concluded from within my self-reliance and my reading of Emerson is that I am smart enough to earn the money (with God's help, of course), and God and I are smart enough to decide at least the *timing* of the outcome of my tithing. Of course, there are many good people who interpret tithing differently. They see it as mandated payments to God's spiritual shepherds."

"I'm fascinated."

"Do you see that book on the shelf over there? It is Henry Lansdell's *The Sacred Tenth, Studies in Tithegiving Ancient and Modern.* My parents acquired a copy of it shortly after it was published in 1906, after Bessie Cooper had suggested that it would be a nice present for my parents to give me. Although Mr. Landsdell is a wee bit too institutionally driven to suit my sense of individualism, he rightly says that tithing: '...is conducive to prosperity...checks extravagance...is an incentive to carefulness...promotes the development of spiritual life.'"

"*The Sacred Tenth*," Robert Anderson repeated as he looked at the spine of the book. "Good title!"

"I firmly believe that it is essential to the core of my self-reliance that I save 10% of every $1.00 I earn, in fact, 10% of every $1.00 that passes through my hands. I am, you see, at that moment tithing for God and me. The *principal* is what I prefer to call the 10%, and the principal may not be touched. Yes, everything is God's, so naturally the principal is His, lies at the very heart of Him, and it will grow, uncorrupted, undiminished by me. The principal will earn its own interest, which from time to time may be made available in plenteous and satisfying amounts for the needs of desperate humans, but not for healthy and less needful intervening religious representatives. You see, young man, I am God's representative. And why not *I?*"

"Descartes," Robert Anderson said, then whistled.

"Yes, 'I think, therefore I am,'" replied Peter. "And I am as honest and as generous as any church's pastor, any church's elder, any church's missionary."

"And yet, Mr. Pence, the church, which is to say, organized religion, has worked down through the ages, diligently and courageously, at times, outrageously, too, to save humans, while at the same time paying a very heavy price, and I don't think that should be so simply ignored."

"Without question. But keep in mind that no church is stronger than its weakest, most mulish member." He relit his pipe and continued before Anderson had a chance to object to the over-simplification.

"When the Popes were collecting their 'Peter's Pence' in England in the 10th century, each household was required to pay a precious penny to Rome. Sounds simple, but it wasn't. The Pope didn't receive all the pennies because some of them stayed in the pockets of the local collectors, some of them stayed in the pockets of the King and some in the trousers of a good many of the King's miscreant men. There were just as many Adams then as there are now. My brother, Adam, was neither the first nor the last to misspend his life. 'Peter's Pence' was inefficient and the ultimate intent behind it was bad enough, but what I have come to understand, young man, is that each one of us acting as an individual should be collecting and administering our *own* 'Peter's Pence.'"

"Damn it...excuse me, darn it...."

"Drat it?" supplied Mr. Pence with a smile.

"Thank you, but I'm going with damn it, this whole pence business is too simple, simplistic, naive, actually. You see, Mr. Pence, we are talking *trillions* these days, and that is tenths to the twelfth power. Our financial space ship is now in *galaxies* of numbers, and pennies are as minuscule as any microscopic quantity imaginable. The answer, it seems to many, will be found by the economic technocrats, those who're convinced that individuals left to their own devices simply cannot or will not resolve the complexities of their dilemma."

"So, we should turn over our individual responsibilities to government or some other system and rely upon technicians to be in charge of our welfare?"

"Yes."

"No."

"Why not?"

"Because technicians don't hang their pants on the wall and run and jump into them every morning. They put them on one leg at a time just like everybody else."

Peter P. Pence reached for his Bible.

"Do not forget the words of St. Luke, IX, 14-17," he sighed as he began to read: "'For they were about five thousand men. And he said to his disciples, Make them sit down by fifties in a company.

"'And they did so, and made them all sit down.

"'Then he took the five loaves and the two fishes, and looking up to heaven, he blessed them, and brake, and gave to the disciples to set before the multitude.

"'And they did eat and were all filled: and there was taken up of fragments that remained to them twelve baskets.'

"To me, the parable emphasizes plainness, which flies in the face of those who spend beyond their means, and who consider a 10% tithe impossible, yet whenever they do tithe, they do it in the wrong way. Discipline yourself to live *within* your means, impose the tithe, and do not give it to middlemen. Remember, Adolph Ochs bought your *New York Times* at auction before either one of us was born, at a time when a multitude of 5,000 technocrats could not have saved it."

"Therefore, you are not presuming to ask me for *my* tithe, I presume?"

"Of course not. I would never do that. You are smart enough to collect your own Peter's Pence and distribute it yourself with God's help. And it is your individual responsibility to do so."

"And yet, Mr. Pence, you seem to be suggesting that there is no need for churches, no need for the worthy ministrations of churches and the good, God-fearing ministers within them, when in fact, without some religious *structure* most of us would revert to living as animals, I'm inclined to believe."

"And many of us would be improved by it," countered Peter P. Pence as he tamped the tobacco into his pipe, re-lit, drew in the smoke and exhaled gently through pursed lips. "Have you been reading the *first* ten commandments?" he wanted to know.

"I have been reading them, yes, but I'm not at all sure that I have been living them," the reporter confessed.

"They are not easy, that is true, but if all anyone does is *read* the great commandments while not trying diligently to *live* them, then it becomes a great hypocrisy, does it not?"

"A waste of time as well?"

"Of course."

"But, why do you suppose God picked these ten? He could have selected 100," Anderson quarreled.

"God, who made Heaven and Earth, can do anything. A long time ago, I made a conscious decision not to argue with God, rather I chose to *work with* God through Faith."

"Otherwise, a waste of time?"

"Not only a waste of time, but disrespectful."

"Pagan?"

"Yes. Consider this: *discipline is the foundation for character.*

"Discipline?"

"Have you thought very much about the word, 'discipline?'

"Self-control?"

"Very good. 'Discipline,' you see, as with disciples, presupposes teaching *and* learning. But neither will amount to a stalk of corn without self-control. And remember, not all of the disciples were perfectly disciplined."

"Judas?"

"Even my great namesake, Peter."

"How do you account for the fact, and I must return to this, how do you account for the fact that there were ten children in your family, yet only you, the tenth, much more than Angie and Pine, came to such a rich understanding about life?"

"I'm not sure. Yet, often I think that harmony in matters of the spirit and music are well-founded upon certain numbers, as in the case of the threes, the great trilogy, for example, and eights as in the tonal octaves, but in matters of financial riches I've come to rely greatly on tens."

"And tens are the primary results of *ones*?"

"Precisely. Without *ones* there can never be *tens*. Your formal education and the fact that you have won a Pulitzer Prize have not ruined you after all. Apparently your organized religion hasn't botched you either," added Peter as he fitted his pipe with a new pinch of burley tobacco grown in his own backyard and cured on the rafters of the small, weathered shed behind his cabin.

"Young man, I should also like to spend some time with you today in order to talk more about *pennies*."

"Oh, *those* ones."

"Oh, yes, *those* ones, as you call them. Do you see this?" he said as he took from the mantlepiece a framed mounting containing three objects: a coin stamped "100 Pesos," a bank note stamped "1,000,000 Pesos," and the words "It happened in Argentina."

"It is exactly this that tells the story of carelessness with unitary amounts, whether they be pennies or pesos. It was sent to me by one of Pine's sons, who was with the Peace Corps in South America. Argentina is not the only country in the western hemisphere to suffer from inflation."

"Mexico?"

"Of course. And the United States of America, too, which was asked in 1995 to put up $20-$40 billion to bail out the pitiful Mexican peso. In each instance, organized religion played a major role to this extent: all those feet of clay in those leather sandals beneath those velvet robes have seldom, it seems to me, seldom if ever instructed young people to save their own Peter's Pence, and apply it *intelligently*. The people typically have failed to make it 'The Sacred Tenth.'"

Peter opened his smaller Bible to St. Matthew: Chapter XVIII, Verse 12. He slowly read: "How think ye? if a man have a hundred sheep, and one of them be gone astray, doth he not leave the ninety and nine, and goeth into the mountains, and seeketh that which is gone astray?"

"We have forsaken the penny?"

"We have forsaken the penny *and* God. We have ignored the cornerstone of our financial house and our spiritual well-being. It was forsaken by individuals in both the North and the South at the time of the American Civil War. In fact, there are many Good Samaritans today who still refuse to stoop to pick up a wayward penny from the sidewalk. Just as many have ignored the sweetest whispers of God.

"Let me tell you how I envision the penny: each one is a soldier in my army."

"A pawn in your crusade?"

"No. Listen to me. One penny quickly becomes 10 pennies and 10 pennies become 100 and 100 pennies become 1,000. I NEVER spend my pennies. They are the real, the founding substance of my principal."

"It's a process, but it's an extremely slow one, and by the way, where do you keep all your pennies?" Robert Anderson suddenly asked.

"There's the root of your generation's problem."

"Too fast?"

"Much too fast. You will never appreciate or obtain great wealth, spiritual as well as physical, until you have come to a reverence for each penny, each soldier in your army in its battle against wastefulness and eventual insolvency. As for where I keep my pennies, I keep them where I can watch them."

"Isn't it a little too late to be picking up pennies from the sidewalk?"

"NO!" boomed Peter P. Pence. "Absolutely, not, it is never too late. This commonwealth of ours, this nation of ours, this world of ours MUST start now to restore the penny to its rightful importance in all we do. If I, Peter P. Pence, can do it *everybody* can do it. If I, Peter P. Pence, can save just *one* penny a day for 70 years, and at the end of that time have 25,550 pennies, or $255.50 anyone not only can do it but should do it. Assuming that there are 250,000,000 people living in the United States and that in their average lifetimes they are living 70 years and each is saving ONLY ONE PENNY a day, the amount adds up to what?"

"You want me to figure it out?" Anderson asked.

"Yes. Take this pencil and this piece of paper and multiply $255.50 times 250,000,000. How much is it?"

Robert Anderson began multiplying.

"It's $63 billion, 875 million, and it's just damn well incredible," Anderson said, shaking his head.

"When you return next Sunday, we will discuss the thirteenth commandment."

"Mr. Pence?"

"Yes."

"I have a grandson I'd like to bring with me. Would that be all right? I mean, I'd like for you to talk with him about pennies."

"By all means. The best habits are formed early."

CHAPTER SIX

Peter was 10 years old, Pine was 20, and Angie was 26 when their mother and father died at the peak of what was called "the best of times for American farmers." The annual report of the Department of Agriculture had placed the value of corn at $1.7 billion, more than "all the gold and silver coin and bullion" in the United States. After the stock market crashes of 1901 and 1907, it was a golden time that helped to create, it was boasted, "the establishment of banks and better homes and helped to make the farmer a citizen of the world." The rhetoric had been inflated, but there'd been just enough truth in it to underpin the public relations campaign, easily selling a picture to a hungry populus not typical by a long shot in the Pocket, though it had most city people believing it.

For Christmas that year, Prudence had given Patience a new pair of overalls. He'd also gone to town and returned with a new pair of brogans to replace the ones beginning to rot around the edges where the cowhide met the soles, allowing cold creek water to seep through and set the stage for pneumonia. He'd given Prudence, old and tired at 44 years, a small bottle of perfume. She'd frowned about it.

Peter was the only child left at home after Pine had gone off to the university on a scholarship he'd earned for "Most Improved and Needful Student." Angie had traveled on her horse deeper into the mountains to bring midwifery to women who had borne their children year after year, young and old women who believed it was their solemn duty to serve the passions of their husbands, no matter the cost, no matter the degradation.

"You'll be just fine," Angie would tell her womenkind, soothing their foreheads with cool, dampened cloths.

"I don' feel just fine," they'd reply. "But praise God you've come," they'd murmur.

"I know. I know. You be just fine. You be just fine."

"Woman," some men would pout, "how come you're just now a-gettin' here?"

"Man," Angie would fire back with courage born of old Daniel and Jacob, Armilda and Suffiah, "you get your sweet ass outta the door, and you leave me and this here woman a-yours ALONE, elsewise, you hain't gonna have no woman nor no baby neither."

On the fourth Sunday of his visits with Peter P. Pence, Robert Anderson brought with him his ten-year-old grandson, Samuel. Anderson knew it was chancy, because the boy lived in a time when video games were played on wide screens, when television was "high definition," when candy bars cost 70 pennies, single dip ice cream cones cost 200 pennies, and toys usually cost about 2,500 pennies. His grandfather warned the boy not to expect any pennies from Peter P. Pence.

"I think you're going to like this interesting old man," Anderson coaxed.

"Why do you think so?" the little boy wanted to know.

"Because you are the future. Mr. Pence will probably say that you are the future. He will say that it's a perfect time in your life to begin saving your pennies."

"But I already do save my pennies," said the child.

"Yes, you do. But you always end up *spending* your pennies," correspondent Anderson countered with grandfatherly kindness.

The boy looked at his father's father and said no more. They flew up from Atlanta to Lexington and rented a car at Blue Grass Airport. Soon they were heading up the Mountain Parkway.

"These aren't such big mountains," said Samuel.

"We're on the western edge of the Appalachians," Anderson replied. "The higher mountains lie mainly to the southeast. These are the foothills, but soon you will see the outline of the mountains on the horizon."

The child retrieved a video game from his backpack and pushed the button triggering a jingle of tones and lighting the miniature screen with two warriors, sabers sparkling, the exaggerated shoulders of the bodies flexing for mortal combat, good guy pitted against bad guy. Samuel extended his ten fingers, limbered his forefingers and placed them on the two buttons, which controlled the good guy's movements. Samuel usually kept score on how many times Mr. Good defeated Mr. Bad, like David slaying Goliath, although Samuel did not usually think in Biblical terms.

"Samuel," said Robert Anderson, "you've played that game most of the way from Atlanta. Would you please put it away now and watch the shapes of the mountains as they appear?"

The child touched the off-button, placed the handset back inside its cover and returned the miniature computer to a pocket in the backpack.

"Grandfather," said Samuel, "do you suppose the people who live here—that house over there—do you suppose they all have computer games?"

"Not all. Some."

"Satellite dishes?"

"Oh, yes, many do. It's the only way they can receive clear signals in remote areas. Only a very few, though, such as my friend, Peter P. Pence, don't have television at all."

"He can't afford it?"

"Oh, he can afford many television sets, satellite dishes, computers, telephones, answering machines, fax machines, laser printers, copying machines, modems, downlinked information from cyberspace. Do you know what cyberspace is, Samuel?"

The child looked kindly at his grandfather. "Yes, Grandfather," he said.

Samuel spent most of his waking hours in the land of Davids and Goliaths clashing on a battleground, their voices in victory making sounds of ecstacy, in defeat the utterance becoming a desperate, choking "Ughhh," a cry that had excited Samuel at first but now had dulled, although deep in his psyche he never lost the desire to hear it one more time.

"Your friend does have a television set," said Samuel, matter of factly.

"No, he doesn't. He doesn't want one. He doesn't have an automobile, either."

"Is he a hermit?"

"Well, yes, you could say that."

"He must be very lonely," sighed Samuel.

Robert Anderson left the parkway at the Crossland exit and headed up the state road toward the Pocket. He parked the car at the foot of the hill, and he and his grandson walked up to the log dogtrot. Anderson knocked on the door and called:

"Mr. Pence?"

"Come in."

"Mr. Pence, this is my grandchild, Samuel."

"Well, well, well, my good man, it's just so good to see you. Please sit over there on that other nail keg, and your grandfather will sit on the one in front of the fireplace, his accustomed place. If you don't mind, I'll sit here in my rocking chair, which has grown so used to me it has taken up the curve in my spine!"

"Mr. Pence, my grandson saves pennies, but I'm encouraging him to hang on to them and not be tempted to spend them on things he really does not need."

"How old are you, Samuel?" said Peter.

"Ten," replied Samuel.

"Good age, good age," said Peter. "Now then, my good man, your grandfather and I have been discussing the Ten Commandments, some of which you should be keeping, one for each year of your life! 'Honour thy father and mother; that thy days may be long upon the land which the Lord thy God giveth thee,'" intoned Peter. "Don't you think that's a good idea?" he asked Samuel.

"Yes sir," he replied. "I mean, I think so."

"Very good. I like young men who *think*. I also like it when young men refer to older men as 'Sir,'" said Peter. "I would return the sign of courtesy and respect to any man who is older than I, but these days there aren't too many who are older than I, so do you know what I do?"

"No, sir."

"I say, 'Sir,' to all men. Do you know what 'Sir' means, Samuel?"

"No, sir."

"It's a shortened version of *sire*. That's a term of the glorious days of chivalry. The knights in King Arthur's roundtable were *sires*. They were addressed as *Sir* Gawain or *Sir* Launcelot, and if Samuel had been among them he would have been called, *Sir* Samuel," said Peter.

"I like that," said Samuel. "I have warriors on my pocket video game."

"Yes. And do you not imagine that the sires would be most careful about how they conserved their strength? To be ready for battles, I mean? And, of course, to defend their lovely ladies."

"Guinevere," smiled Samuel as he cupped his chin on the base of his hand and with his elbow anchored on his leg above his knee, fastened his eyes on Peter P. Pence and waited for more.

"There are many sources of strength. I will name some for you. The first two are fundamental: health in body and soul. That means healthy, responsible *individualism*. Everything falls into line after that. The next source of strength for King Arthur and his knights of the roundtable in Camelot in the 6th century, as well as for Sir Samuel and Sir Peter on this last month of the 20th century, is health in matters of money management. Do you know what I mean, Samuel, when I say, 'money management'?"

"I suppose it means—it means, taking care of the coins in your pocket?"

"Oh, yes. It means knowing, too, how the coins came to be in your pocket in the first place. It also means knowing what to do with them once they're there."

"My grandfather says I save my pennies, but then I spend my pennies."

"Do you?"

"I suppose I do," said Samuel as he shifted hands to hold his chin.

"Let me talk with you and your grandfather about what I call the thirteenth commandment. It is a money management strategy I have devised and, for me, it has worked exceedingly well. I have known of no one else who has tried it. Perhaps you, Samuel, will become the second after me.

"Thou shalt impose the 10% SELF TAX."

"What's the difference between the '10% Self Tax' and tithing?" Robert Anderson interjected from his nail keg. "Tithing for oneself, of course," he hastily added.

"The 10% Self Tax is an additional amount imposed on each *expense*. For example, each $1.00 spent must have attached to it an additional 10 cents, which you then place immediately into the principal. Samuel, let us begin with a $2.00 serving of ice cream. What's your favorite flavor?"

"Butter pecan."

"Strawberry is mine. Now, Samuel, you have just given the ice cream worker *three* one-dollar bills."

"But it only costs two dollars, and I have the two one-dollar bills."

"Why do you hand over the third one-dollar bill?"

"Yes, sir, I would like to know that."

"Because you are pretending that the ice cream cost $2.20 and you need the change for one dollar in order to put two dimes into your left pocket. Are you right-handed, Samuel?"

"Yes, sir."

"Fine. Then your right pocket is for the spending side of you, and your left pocket is for the saving side of you. The clerk will probably tell you that you've handed over too much, but you will say, 'I need the change, please. Would you mind giving me three quarters, two dimes and a nickel?'"

Samuel seemed so fascinated he placed his hands on his knees, straightened himself and leaned closer to Mr. Pence.

"Now what do I do?" he asked.

"Always remember, you are taxing yourself 10%. Even if the clerk adds 12 cents in state tax to the original $2.00, raising the total cost of the ice cream to $2.12, you apply your 10% self tax, which now becomes 21 cents. You have handed over the three one-dollar bills, and the clerk returns 88 cents in change. Place two dimes in your left pocket along with *all* of the pennies, in this case, three—*always* save your pennies. *Never* spend your pennies. Later, you will learn to *invest* your pennies."

"It sounds like a lot of trouble, meaning no offense, sir," said Samuel.

"Sounds like it, but it isn't. It's as easy and as fun and as profitable as tying your shoestrings each morning so you won't trip and fall on your face," smiled Peter P. Pence. "You know, Samuel and Mr. Anderson, our nation, I think, has forgotten to tie its shoestrings, and it's about to fall on its face!"

"Mr. Pence, would you give me an example of a situation in which the stakes are higher than $2.00?" Robert Anderson interposed.

"All right, on a larger scale, let us say that you wish to purchase an automobile for $20,000 (personally, I'm flabbergasted by the amounts being paid for automobiles in this decade), but now you must add $2,000 to the price of the car. That amount is the self-tax. If you do not have the $2,000, you must arrange to borrow $22,000. If you cannot afford to pay or borrow the larger amount, then you cannot afford the original amount. This is how the self-tax works as a second governor on the speed of your spending."

"You would have me pay additional interest on the extra $2,000? I don't see the wisdom in that."

"When you place the $2,000 in your principal it will earn offsetting interest. Although it will not equal the interest charged on the $2,000, it will substantially lower it, and the governor will still be working like a charm."

"In a sense, then, I will be borrowing an additional $2,000 and I will be *investing* it?"

"Yes. Some investors frequently rely upon borrowed funds in order to purchase stocks on margin, and although I don't recommend it as a normal procedure, when used in the way I have described, it is a good use of the money, and potentially a profitable one. However, I would *not* use the borrowed money to buy speculative stock."

"Conservative investments?"

"No other kind. Only the bluest of the blue chips."

"Would this work for local, state, and national government?" Anderson asked, as Samuel went to browse among the shelves of books behind Mr. Pence.

"Without doubt. Samuel, you will find a delightful little book over there called, *A Day No Pigs Would Die.* If you start to read it, you may not be able to put it down. It's the story of a young Quaker lad," said Peter as he turned his attention back to the *New York Times* correspondent. "Let's say, the governmental entity has decided to spend $100 million of our money, yours and mine. Why then shouldn't the government spend $110 million and add the additional $10 million to the national principal? Even better, use the extra $10 million to reduce the national deficit, or better still, pay on a debt—DEBT REDUCTION LEADS TO DEFICIT CORRECTION. Yet, again, if the government cannot justify the expenditure of the $110 million, it should not attempt to rationalize the spending of the original $100 million. What they might do, therefore, would be to cut the spending by 10%. Thus, the new expenditure could be $90 million."

"They would have to remember that the actual amount would be $99 million, because the $9 million self-tax of that amount would be headed for the principal, possibly the debt, eventually the deficit," Anderson calculated.

"Now you're cooking," declared Peter. "In fact, instead of building another fighter plane or packing another case of bayonets, it might be prudent to postpone the project by not spending anything at all."

"Depends on what the enemy is building," the reporter cautiously judged.

"Yes it does. Timing is everything. I'm not a pacifist, yet consider the possibility of a more peaceful strategy. The government decides *not* to build the plane—it could nonetheless *imagine* it had built it: take the $100 million and apply the whole amount to the principal or the deficit."

"Plus $10-million for the tax on imagination!" Anderson cried.

"Bravo!" said Peter P. Pence. "Out-of-control spending is no different from my brothers, Adam and Poplar, letting greed and drinking get out of control. Government spenders often remind me of drunken sailors."

"We must go, Mr. Pence. Samuel, what do you think of *A Day No Pigs Would Die?*"

"I think I would like to save a cow's life by helping her deliver her calf. And I would like the owner of the cow to give me a pig as my reward," said Samuel.

"Samuel," said Peter, "I do not have a pig to give you, but I have this fine 1865 Indian head penny. It's worth even more than the $15.00 a collector would be willing to pay you. I would be most pleased if you would take this penny and decide with your grandfather's help the place where it would be safest to keep it."

"Thank you, sir. And I won't spend it on ice cream!"

"You're a splendid thinker, Samuel."

"I have another idea," said Samuel.

"What is that?" replied Peter.

"I'll hand this penny down to my grandchild."

"God willing," said Peter P. Pence.

"May I read here too?" asked Samuel.

"As much as you like," said Peter. "I think you'll enjoy reading about my own Knights of the Round Table," he added.

"Oh, yes," said Samuel.

CHAPTER SEVEN

I am ready, I think, for the fourteenth commandment," Robert Anderson said as he took his seat on the nail keg.

"*Thou shalt not spend thy principal*," intoned Peter P. Pence.

"You might *need* to. The state might need to. The federal government might need to," Anderson objected.

"Disgusting."

"What is disgusting? A *need* is disgusting? Not all needs are disgusting," the reporter pouted.

"What I find so repugnant is your generation's bulging complaint box: 'I *need* this.' 'I *need* that.' 'I *need* you to do this,' and 'I *need* you to do that for me.' Excuse me, young man, but we have inherited and suckled a generation continually in *need* of something. Frankly, I don't think many of you understand what a real *need* is."

"What is a real need, then?" Anderson fired back, but feebly.

"A real need is *not* to win the lottery."

"What's wrong with winning the lottery?"

"Only one thing is worse than winning the lottery, and that is to buy a lottery ticket."

"Even if you knew it was the winning ticket? Come on now, Mr. Pence."

"You come on now, Mr. Anderson. Entire lives have been eaten alive by winning the lottery. Infinitely more lives have been nibbled to death by buying lottery tickets. It is madness. It is as crude as it is thoughtless. It bypasses everything that I am saying about managing money—not spending more than one earns, taking 10% off the top and adding it to the principal, imposing the 10% self-tax and adding it to the principal, and finally, not touching the principal—and to do otherwise is to delude the masses of the people, failing to educate them concerning the acquisition of real worth, while at the same time allowing government to get off the hook of responsibility for the similar actions it should be taking."

"I should tear up my lottery ticket, then," said Anderson, sheepishly pulling it from his pocket.

"Tear it up and throw it into the fireplace," replied Peter Pence.

"Even if it were the winning 'powerball' ticket?" asked Anderson.

"Especially if it were that," said Peter.

Robert Anderson tore the ticket in half and added it to the flames. He wondered for an instant if it might have been the winning $10-million ticket. The stub quickly disappeared in a small, bright flash. Anderson turned and smiled at Peter Pence, and the old man smiled back.

"*Need* #1 is to live by the Ten Commandments. *Need* #2 is to live by the additional commandments I have discussed with you, which will take care of *need* #3: save ourselves from financial ruin. Consider the meaning of the word, principal. Over there you will find one of my friends, the leather-bound *Oxford English Dictionary*. I use it on special occasions. You will need this magnifying glass, for the text is micrographically reproduced. Look up and read to me the meaning of the word, *principal*."

Correspondent Anderson took down into both his hands the huge, black, gold embossed, 1478-1978 volume. He opened it coincidentally to the page headed by "profitful" then worked his way back: "profanatic," "process," "probableness," "privisant," "prismatical," to "principal."

"Origin, source; source of action," said Anderson as he looked up from the magnifying glass, leaving it as a bookmark in the exquisitely printed volume.

"Go on," said Peter P. Pence.

"Fountainhead; original or initial state."

"There is more," Mr. Pence insisted.

"That from which something takes its rise, originates, or is derived. A fundamental source from which something proceeds; a primary element, force or law which produces or determines particular results; the ultimate basis upon which the existence of something depends."

"The ultimate basis upon which the existence of something depends," murmured Peter, "Now, while you are there in the 'Ps' please read to me what is there under 'Peter-penny,' and 'Peter's Penny' and 'Peter's Pence.'"

Anderson was stimulated by the feel of the large pages of words barely discernible with the naked eye. He balanced the large volume on his knees, slowly leafing his way toward his destination.

"'An annual tax or tribute of a penny from each householder having land of a certain value, paid before the Reformation to the Papal See at Rome....It was discontinued by statute in 1534.'"

"Also look at the entries for 'penny,'" said Mr. Pence.

"There are many pages to describe 'penny,'" Anderson discovered.

"Yes. Just consider the entry for Phrases and Proverbs," urged Peter.

"'A penny for your thoughts....A penny in the forehead....A penny saved is a penny gained....A penny sold never came to twopence....A pretty penny....In for a penny, in for a pound....No penny, no paternoster.... Take care of the pennies and the pounds will take care of themselves.'"

"Stop right there, for you have found it. You have found the key to the secret for opening the door to wealth. Now I ask you, why would anybody want to throw that key away? Or if seen lying upon the sidewalk, why would anyone not stoop to pick it up and use it?" asked Peter P. Pence.

"The problem is that we are much too far down the road to be reinventing wheels, picking up pennies or dwelling on moments after decades have passed us by," argued Robert Anderson. "How about 'penny-wise, pound-foolish'? That doesn't seem to be here."

"All right, for the moment let us accept your conclusion, shallow and uninspired as it certainly is," said Peter. "Which is better? Rethinking the issue or refusing to re-evaluate the present dilemma?"

"I think I'm supposed to be asking the questions," said the reporter who had used this tactic many times before.

"Your reply may have worked elsewhere, but it won't cut hot butter here in the Pocket. That is one of the major problems with late 20th century journalism: it wants to run yet another flimsy question up the flagpole and let everybody else take a flying leap for the answer and be responsible for the outcome, and then be ridiculed for appearing awkward or inconsistent. I have a perfect right to ask you, Mr. Anderson of the *New York Times*, what do *you* think?"

"I think you are a very smart man. I think you are the most remarkable man I've ever met. I think your ideas should be part of every school curriculum. I think..."

"So, you think my ideas should be studied?"

"Yes, I do."

"Then for God's sake why don't you say so in your newspaper?"

"Mr. Pence, I am a reporter. I don't believe in taking positions."

"I see. So you stand by and watch your own country go to hell in a hand basket? You were there at Perryville. You were there at Chateau Thierry. You were there at Pearl Harbor. You were there at Auschwitz. You were there at Saigon. You were there in Rwanda. You were there in Oklahoma City. You will be there when the enemy breaks down the door of your house, and all you will do is report it?"

"Mr. Pence, you are now trespassing."

"Yes, I am, and I'm going to take a leap of faith that you can sit there and take it when I tell you that there is no perfection anywhere. Reporters will always be needed to identify the imperfections. But if all you do is report the imperfections, and if all you do is make it your business to ignore the honest attempts in the direction of perfections, then, Mr. Anderson, you and your friends in the news media are no more than buzzards circling the battlefields. Yes, I understand that buzzards have an essential role to play in picking the bones of the dead, and surgeons have a role to play in amputating arms and legs in order to save lives, but journalists also have a responsibility to be human beings first, because in fact they're stuck with it, and they cannot escape that reality. They ARE human beings first and they can ONLY be journalists second."

"Mr. Pence: truce."

"Yes. We will make this our Appomattox."

"Your officers may keep their horses and return home with them for spring plowing."

"You are most generous, General Anderson, most generous indeed."

The sky above the dogtrot was like buttermilk poured in the coolness of the above-ground cellar when Jacob and Daniel paused there on a hot afternoon in the summer of '65.

"She's over," said Daniel.

"She damned well never should'a started," said Jacob.

"Then, why did we fight?" asked Daniel.

"Dammed if I know."

"Mebbe," said Daniel, "mebbe, hit was money, money pure and simple."

"Mebbe."

"Look at this $10 note with Jeff's picture on hit. Hain't worth nothin'."

"Dan'l," said Jake, "money'll always be the problem. 'Specially wild-cat money. Money is as money does, as our pappy always said."

"So, Jake, what we got is ourselves? Me, mebbe short a laig, and you, mebbe short a arm, but what's left of us is all we got, and we best be makin' the most of hit."

Daniel placed his hand on Jacob's shoulder and said what he'd been wanting to say for the past four years: "I'm sorry. We really made a big mess, didn't we?"

Jacob dug deep into his overalls and pulled out a small purse. From it he took a shiny, new, two-cent piece and handed it to Daniel. It was the first coin in the United States to bear the words: "In God We Trust."

"Mine to keep?" said Daniel.

"Yours to keep," said Jacob.

"I should like for you to take a short walk with me, young man," said Peter to Robert Anderson. "There's something down by the barn that I would like you to see."

They walked out onto the dogtrot, and Pumpkin was eager to follow. She ran in small circles with her head angled, so she could keep an eye on her master, cutting him looks and sending him messages of "Whither thou goest..." She was connected to Peter P. Pence like lichen on a water maple, green and crusty, unwilling to let go. Peter pursed his lips and made the sweet, scraping sound that caused Pumpkin's eyes to glaze with ecstasy. She quickly squatted and tinkled.

"What I'm going to show you is the corncrib," said Peter to Robert Anderson. "It's not, I imagine, like any corncrib you've ever seen before."

The building, about 75 yards from the house, was bowed like an old swayback, and the rusty hinges on the doors creaked in the movement of the December wind. Peter opened the side door and walked inside. Anderson was close behind. Pumpkin went off sniffing for cats. The area in which the two men stood was filled with sunlight. The 6 X 12 log beams were notched at their ends and tightly fitted, snug in their 90-degree corners.

"The church," said Peter.

"The church?" asked Robert.

"The Rock Ledge Church," said Peter. "All that's left of it."

"I don't understand."

"My father bought the building the year I was born, dragged the logs here and built a corncrib."

"Was he getting even with the preacher? The one who said it was God's retribution against your brother, Paul?"

"Oh, I doubt it. But maybe. The fact is, these hand-hewn logs outlasted all the congregations. The fact is, any church will be worth no more than an empty corncrib if the people for whatever reason walk away because they no longer feel bonded to fundamental beliefs. At the same time, a corncrib will lose its value if it is not properly stored with grain for the nourishment of God's creatures."

"Mr. Pence, I should like to ask you about *your* faith."

"What is the question?" said Peter as he sat on the doorsill of the corncrib. Pumpkin came in tight between his legs, and Peter rubbed behind the dog's short ears. He was looking for ticks, but it was only a summer habit of winter.

"What does *Faith* personally mean to you?" repeated Anderson.

"It means that if this dog with her absolute trust in me should wander away or die, and if you should weary of me and return to Atlanta and never return to the Pocket, I would not be alone."

"Whom would you have?"

"I would have myself and I would have my innermost voice."

"What is your 'innermost' voice?"

"I'm glad you've asked me this question here in the corncrib, which used to be a church. Now there is no church. There is no choir. There is no priest. There are no sacraments. There is no central authority. I cannot even ask you to consult my books, because I have no books here in the corncrib. There are only the three of us—you, this dog and I. But, for the sake of the discussion, I've removed you and the dog. Do you actually believe that if the Pope, the Archbishop of Canterbury, the chief rabbi, and the heads of all Christian and non-Christian religions in the world were to disappear in a blinding flash, that I would also necessarily disappear because I have no Faith? How utterly silly. Of course, I would have Faith. The golden secret is that I have faith that I would still have Faith. It is helpful, many times, to have a creed, a belief, an organized structure for religion, yet as long as I have my individual intellect, I have all the Faith I will ever need. Others might run around in total despair, but I would not. The problem is as follows, Correspondent Anderson, and you too, Pumpkin, should you care to listen: human beings throughout the world have been conditioned to believe that they are helpless, yea, *faithless*, if the church structures should crumble. Before

the structure of the Rock Ledge Church collapsed and began to decompose, Patience Pence bought the logs, brought them home and built this corncrib. Now, 100 years later, I am sitting here answering your question, 'What does Faith personally mean to you?' It means to me that I was created in the image of God. What does image mean? Its meaning rings true in Yeats' The Indian Upon God:

"'Who made the world and ruleth it, He hangeth on a stalk,
 For I am in His image made, and all this tinkling tide
 Is but a sliding drop of rain between his petals wide.'

"However, Faith unaccompanied by work—I do not mean 'good works' in a narrow, religious sense, but shirking from just plain work— will greatly weaken the house in which Faith makes its home. Be sure to read Emerson's 'Self-Reliance,'" said Peter:

"'There is a time in every man's education when he arrives at the
 conviction that...no kernel of nourishing corn can come to him but
 through his toil bestowed on that plot of ground given to him as a
 place to be.'"

Robert Anderson picked up a corncob and slowly turned it in his hands. He sighted down the rows of pockets where kernels of corn had been attached. He blew his breath against the sheath of shucks at the base of the cob. He rubbed it against the side of his face.

"You are, at this moment, Mr. Anderson, very close to God," said Peter P. Pence as he rested his forehead on his right hand, family images flooding the valleys of remembrance.

After his mother and father had passed on, Peter had gone to town and bought a safe-deposit box, the key to which he had fastened to a simple chain, and which he then hung around his neck. In the life of Peter P. Pence, Bessie Cooper and others had said, it was as if at least some of the badness had begun to pass, as if God Himself had at last grown tired and intervened to put an end to so much misery in one family. Patience and Prudence had had ten years of relative calm, an inner contentment in which Peter had played a major part. He had not made trouble. He had loved, and he had worked—driving the wagons loaded with freshly ground limestone in summer, holding the reins of the horses hauling corn from the fields in fall, "geeing" and "hawing" the ice blocks from the pond in winter, keeping the animals fed and bedded, pulling the calves and the lambs when mothers couldn't deliver, plowing, harrowing and dragging the topsoil for tobacco, burning the beds for plants, cutting, housing, and stripping the burley leaf, threshing the hemp—and he had taken mighty good care of his mother and father too. Peter had encouraged Pine to study to become a doctor, and Peter had comforted Angie whenever, rare as it was, she'd return from the mountains, another worn-out woman sacrificing her own life that other women and their babies might stand a better chance to survive, yet not just survive, but to live with hope as the Apostle Paul had written.

When the midnight hour came for Patience and Prudence to go Home, as they always called it and loved it and trusted it, their hearts simply stopped beating, Patience's first, then Prudence's, within one hour of each other. Night fell on the burning bush, its cinders blowing away.

On the day of the funeral for Patience and Prudence, Peter, only 10 years old, yet acting and seeming much older, had sat for a time at the kitchen table with Angie and Pine, and he had spoken with them directly.

"I know I'm the baby. I know I'm nowhere near legal age. But I have a secret, which I'm willing to share with you at least in part. I'm only ten years old, and Angie, you are 26. Pine, you are 20. These numbers are not important. They are just numbers. Angie, you give me another ten years, and I'll see to it that you have your clinic for mothers in the mountains. Pine, you give me another ten years, and I'll see to it that your medical school expenses have been paid in full. That's all I can tell you right now. I want you to trust me. I want you to believe in me. I want you to leave me be here where I belong—in the dogtrot.

"Angie, I want you to go back to the mountains and keep on

working for all those women who need your help, and Pine, I want you to become the doctor you say you want to be, and I want you to save as many people as possible from heavy drinking. I want each one of us to do what we can in our own ways to make the living of our parents, Patience and Prudence, not to have been in vain."

Angie and Pine looked at each other, then looked at Peter. Pine was the first to speak.

"Peter, you've got the ten years and more if you need them. You belong here. I don't. I'm willing to see what happens."

"God bless you, Peter," was all that Angie said.

It was Peter, the man-child becoming much more man than child, it seemed, who saw to the burying of Patience and Prudence near the locust thicket up behind the dogtrot, built to withstand the cold of January ice caps, the storms of March winds, the drinking of moonshine likker, and all the ridge running any wayward youth might undertake. It was Easter time, and spring was showing itself in the way the robins were wrestling worms up and out of the swelling earth. Dogwoods were blooming in profusion.

There was a crowd of neighbors from many households in the Pocket. Bessie was there, of course, and Angie lowered her head and said a prayer that all God's women would have a better chance to bear their children and at the same time keep their health.

Paula had gone to California. The last heard from her had been a perfume-y, jerkily written comic postcard from her dressing room table at a San Francisco dance hall. The card made a crude comparison between a bare-breasted woman and a Jersey cow.

Adam, who had grown up stubborn, vicious as a water moccasin, too mean for anything as pleasant as alcoholism to have had the slightest effect on his mean-spirited nature, always harbored disdainful, strange and deep contempt for his family, especially "Baby Peter." A gambling man from Cincinnati to Indianapolis and on to Chicago, Adam always

wore his felt hat rakishly affected in a downward slant to the left side of his high cheekbone, shoes gleaming with polish so bright it acted as a mirror clearly reflecting any image daring to intrude inside its territory. Adam returned from time to time to the Pocket, though, as if drawn to it despite all his affectations, as if needing sizable hunks of the hillbillies, craving their adoring fascination with his success "up there" in the north. Usually, Adam frightened good people, and they generally avoided him.

"Adam's in the Pocket," they'd whisper, and every man, woman and child would know exactly what that meant—a time for the biddies to see to the gathering of their chicks about them, flustering, "kerrrrwracking," feathering them in under their wings for protection.

"Adam's gone from the Pocket," they'd say, and the biddies would go off clucking, "ccrrrackkk," the children free to venture out again, though doubtless there were many more young girls and more old hens than anyone was willing to admit who were attracted by the hat and the shoes and the diamond stickpin gleaming from the middle of the tie splashed with colors. If truth were known, there were mothers themselves who felt a tingling in their toes and fingertips whenever Adam was in the Pocket.

Adam had come back at age 24 in time to see his mother and father lowered into their graves. Peter had never forgotten and was hard-pressed to forgive how his brother had picked up a handful of dirt and had slung it violently against the closing ground.

"All your damn fault," he had scolded, stomping to his waiting Tin Lizzy, seizing the crank, jerking it up with a snapping vengeance, jumping inside, and rattle-trapping away, spitting gravel like a hail-devil would, never to be seen again by Peter or anybody else in the Pocket neck of the woods. It was Adam's habit to blame others for all misfortunes. The mob gunned him down six months later in Gary, leaving his body to rot on the Indiana sand dunes.

Each detail of the family's life had been recorded in journals by Peter, and each day without fail he had filled up the pages of the red-cloth ledgers, beginning in 1907, when he was seven years old and

Bessie Cooper had urged him to begin the journal-keeping. Likewise, Bessie had encouraged Peter to keep a minutely itemized accounting of each of his expenditures and each of his earnings, so that on any given day he knew exactly what was his to have and to hold. He left out nothing. He put in the stories his mother and father had passed along from their mothers and fathers: the last day of the slaughter at Perryville; Jacob's and Daniel's long walk home together; the reunions with Suffiah and Armilda. The birthing of Patience and Prudence and their marriage and how they'd dreamed of better days.

The journals were all in the local library as the 21st century began. Bessie long ago had passed on, Angel had died when she was 50 years old, but there was in the mountains a thriving "Angel's Rest" for obstetrics and pediatric care, and Dr. Robert "Pine" Pence had spent his life of 75 years, rising to the presidency of the American Medical Association and earning a nomination for the Nobel Prize for his research into the mysteries of alcoholism.

Pine's children: Thomas, named for Poplar; Angelina, named for Angie; and Peter, named for his uncle, had each become teachers living in both North and South, and some of their grandchildren might have gathered each year at the dogtrot in the Pocket to commemorate their heritage if they'd cared.

Just as Peter P. Pence would want it, each year's volume of journals was easily available for anyone with a serious purpose, a desire to know more about the 19th and 20th centuries through the eyes and ears of a little boy, through his growing-up time to manhood and finally to elderly status. Visitors to the dogtrot would talk about it, and they had come to an increased understanding of the importance of family records, both the good and the bad but especially the bad, because from it would come the best learned lessons. Peter P. Pence was as true to his journal as the sun rising each morning over the Pocket, more valuable than all the gold and silver in the world.

Peter had never married, although he had had many opportunities with young ladies and older widows who knew that unlike Adam, Peter was exceedingly gentle and had become a mysteriously wealthy man too, relatively speaking, depending on how one counts wealth. Peter lived all of his life in the same log house where he was born and where he expected to die, but not before the year 2000. All his days he had imagined he would become a centenarian, had conditioned himself to think in that way. He had profited from his own mistakes, to be sure, but he knew he had profited much more greatly from the errors of his brothers and sisters.

CHAPTER EIGHT

C harlie," said Robert Anderson, "I'm going to need more time."
"I knew it. Always the same. Never changes. Can't go out and do a nice quick and dirty interview with an old man without drowning in answers," said the editor of the *New York Times* over the cellular phone in Robert Anderson's car.

"Charlie, you've been getting my faxes?"

"Yes, and it's the only thing that's saving your ass, not to mention your job."

"What do you think?"

"I think we're stuck with him. Good copy. Clean. Well written. Shit, man, what do you expect me to say?"

"Thank you."

"Don't get carried away. Remember, we're paying you to do a job."

"Sure, Charlie. Might even win another Pulitzer."

"Unfair, unfair. If you can't play fair, don't play."

"Chill out, Charlie."

"Listen Mr. Pulitzer or Mr. Hearst or whatever in hell your name is—we're putting together the biggest issue in *New York Times* history. If you want Mr. Pence in it, and if you want a job in the new century, you'll keep sending the faxes and you'll wrap this puppy up, so we can find something else for you to do."

"Charlie."

"Yeah?"

"Never mind."

Robert Anderson sat on the nail keg for the sixth successive Sunday in front of the fireplace in Peter Pence's log house. The reporter had been wondering what was over in the other half of the dogtrot. The old man had never offered to show him. Maybe it was filled with junk. Maybe antiques. Maybe cyberspace. Maybe nothing. Anderson decided not to ask as soon as possible.

"Mr. Pence, I've been wondering what would happen if everybody saved one penny a day and added it to the principal."

"It would not solve everything," said Peter P. Pence. "Permit me to fix us our Sunday breakfast."

The old man took a loaf of bread from the cupboard, and he sliced generous portions. "My mother, Prudence, gave me the recipe for homemade salt rising bread, and I've become rather attached to it," said Peter. He made clean slices with a long, serrated bread knife.

"Although each penny is a soldier in the army of our protection, we need good generals. More than that, we need strong, right-thinking citizens to explain to the generals what the mission means," said Peter as he added coffee to the top of the tin percolator on the stove.

"There will always be neighborhood thieves, as there will always be international rogues. The mission is to protect the principal from them, true, but equally as important we will need protection from our *selves*."

"That's a paradox!" Anderson worried, loudly.

"Yes, it certainly is and always will be. And the reason is that there IS no perfection in this life, no ultimate truth in this earthly life. There is propaganda, and it will always be used and abused by those who wish to seize the principal."

"And the power that goes with it."

"Exactly. The principal IS power. So, the question becomes, how best to protect the principal and its accompanying potency. It is my judgment that the best hope lies within accumulated and coordinated *individualism*."

"You're beginning to sound like a communist," Anderson smiled.

"I hope not."

"Socialist?"

"Wrong again. The United States of America and the political, economic and social system it represents is unquestionably one of the wonders of the world. It is not always right, but the opportunity to *be* right always exists within capitalism."

"How do you define *capitalism*?"

"Look in the *American Heritage*, and you will find as good a definition as any: 'An economic system in which the means of production and distribution are privately or corporately owned and development is proportionate to the accumulation and reinvestment of profits gained in a free market.'

"The rich taking advantage of the poor."

"Young man, I usually don't speak with vulgarity. But there is also a definition for 'bullshit' in the *American Heritage*. If you expect to have breakfast with me, you will kindly look up the word 'bullshit' and read it back to me as I take out the butter and strawberry preserves."

Correspondent Anderson looked up the word and read it aloud: "'Bullshit: foolish, insolent talk; nonsense. To engage in idle conversation. To attempt to mislead or deceive by talking nonsense.'"

"While you're about it, check the meaning of 'horse shit,'" said Peter P. Pence as he set the table for breakfast.

"'Horse shit: meaningless or insincere talk or action; nonsense.' May I still join you for breakfast?" he asked.

"Yes, you may."

"The bread is very good. It's light but has substance," Anderson said.

"You began today by asking me what would happen if everybody would save one penny and add it to the principal, I believe?"

"Yes sir."

"How many people are there in the world today, would you guess?"

"About 6,000,000,000, of which in the United States of America alone there are an estimated 250,000,000."

"And multiplying faster than we are able to count," said Mr. Pence. "Let's play a game. Let's cut the world population in half to account for earthquakes, hurricanes and calamities of all kinds. Let's project the result of 3,000,000,000 people saving one penny a day and adding it to the principal."

"Everybody living an average of 70 years?"

"Yes."

"Well, you would first multiply 365 by 70, and that would equal 25,550. That's the total number of pennies for each individual. Multiply that total by 3,000,000,000, and that would give the world a principal of 76,650,000,000,000 pennies. Converted to dollars, that would be $766,500,000,000. That's an incredible amount of money."

"And all the result of *half* of the people in the world living to be 70 years old and saving only *one* penny each day of their lives.

"You see," said Peter P. Pence, "I've never forgotten my William Wordsworth, who, it is noted in the *Oxford Companion to English Language*, 'left the university without distinction:'

> *"The world is too much with us, late and soon,*
> *Getting and spending we lay waste our powers.*
> *Little we see in Nature that is ours:*
> *We have given our hearts away, a sordid boon!'*

"The fact that so many have not read Wordsworth, and so many of those who have do not see the simple wisdom in his writing, they spend most of their lives on an endless treadmill of working in order to spend more and more and more to buy more and more and more, while all the time there are infinite possibilities to 'see in nature' what is 'ours,' and it is all FREE."

"But, that's capitalism!"

"Indeed. And I support it, yet I believe there can be and ought to be more *responsible* and *sensitive* capitalistic practices."

"Contradiction in terms."

"Not at all. You are buying into cynicism."

"All right, then what are some examples of *free* possibilities within a more responsible and sensitive capitalism?" Robert Anderson asked, anticipating what many of them would be.

"Sunsets, sunrises, seasons, the lives of birds, the lives of squirrels laying by for winter, the lives of spiders weaving webs, unfettered friendships, fresh air, clean water, landscapes: I've given you ten. You could find ten more. Would you like to try?" asked Peter P. Pence, as he buttered another piece of salt rising bread and generously spread strawberry preserves on it, crust to crust.

"The lives of bees making honey, the lives of rabbits staying away from hawks, the lives of buzzards circling for carrion, the lives of sheep circling for warmth, the lives of dogs loving their masters, the lives of crickets rubbing their legs, the lives of lightning bugs flashing signals, the lives of gardens, the lives of trees, the life of you, Peter P. Pence, the tenth on my list of nature's wonders...

> "'So might I, standing on this pleasant lea,
> Have glimpses that would make me less forlorn;
> Have sight of Proteus rising from the sea,
> Or hear old Triton blow his wreathed horn.'

"Ah, you, too, know your Wordsworth!" exclaimed Peter P. Pence.

"There's something I want to ask you, sir."

"So far you've not been shy about asking questions."

"What's in the rooms on the other side of the dogtrot?"

"I wondered when you would ask. I'm glad you finally have. I'll be happy to show you. It is my special reading room. It's where I save and savor material and spiritual wealth. Would you like to see it?"

"Yes, I would."

"Then you shall see it. Come with me." Mr. Pence led Robert Anderson out the door, across the passageway and into the other side.

"You will find many books here. I never throw one away, no matter how bad it might be."

"You seem to have enough nailkegs."

"Oh, yes, they are convenient for sitting or for standing and reaching to the higher shelves. Perhaps someone will come here and catalogue these books and pamphlets, periodicals and newspapers. I seem to know where everything is, but those who follow after me will have great difficulty."

"Who is there to follow you?" asked Anderson.

"In fact, no one. Perhaps, some of Pine's descendants will show an interest in it, but so far they've not."

"Sometimes, families are the poorest source for continuity. I do not know why that is true," said Anderson.

"Oh, it is not unlike a poet in his own country. 'Like a Poet hidden in the light of thought, singing hymns unbidden, til the world is wrought to sympathy with hopes and fears it headed not.'"

"Who is that?"

"Shelley. He is here. And Milton. And Shakespeare. They are all among the occupiers of this side of the dogtrot. Mr. Anderson, it seems to me that it is literature that has made the difference, beginning in my life as early and as sweetly primitive as McGuffey's *Eclectic Reader* and cutting across my ten decades to fellow-Kentuckian Wendell Berry's *What are People For?*"

Robert Anderson counted the nailkegs—there were ten—in the room filled with books. It was as if he had entered a giant intellect, where knowledge lined labyrinthine lanes of pages, upon which words played a game of understanding, more often serious, but tragicomic too; the possibilities were infinite.

"They're all connected, the books, I mean," said Peter P. Pence. "You asked about my faith. You see, my God-given intellect is not satisfied with council-approved creeds, apostolic successions or religious tracts alone. Yes, it would be possible for me to have spent my entire 100 years with nothing more than Prudence and Patience's Parallel Bible. There is enough there in God's word to have sustained me, caused me to have been born again and finally saved me for Heaven above. Yet, the humanity in me, yes, the Adam in me—as bad as he was in our family—has tempted me to seek even richer understanding through the expansion and the increased sensitivity of my thinking through reading."

"Why have recent generations so shunned good reading, if that's the right word for it?"

"One word: *television*. Another: *advertising*. Another: *sports*. Then: *short attention span*. Here's another wrong kind of trilogy: *drugs, sex, violence*. Three growing out of the first three: *loss of values*. Another trinary set: *laziness, indifference, greed*. Three words growing out of the first three: *loss of spirit*."

"Mr. Pence, assuming your assumptions are correct, what is the alternative? What can untelevised, un-advertised, unsports-related, longer-attention-spanned, valued and spirited people do to turn civilization around, especially when they live in a capitalist society?"

"Draw up a nailkeg."

"It's very heavy," said Robert Anderson.

"Turn it on its bottom edge and leverage it in any direction you wish to go."

Anderson complied. Peter maneuvered one of the kegs so as to face the reporter.

"Now then. First things first, as Eric Hoffer said. The world, which is to say *civilization*, unlike a simple, isolated nailkeg, will not be 'turned around.' It will continue to move forward, perhaps two steps forward and one step backward, but forward nonetheless. A nation that can survive divisiveness on the magnitude of the American Civil War CAN go forward. On that day in October, 1862, when Jake and Daniel came home together to this dogtrot in the Pocket, it was living proof of the words: 'United We Stand, Divided We Fall.'"

"Could there not also be an argument that '*United We Fall?*'" asked Correspondent Anderson. "Jonestown comes to mind. And Waco, Texas. And the Third Reich. And poison gas on a Japanese subway."

"Yes, indeed. It is quite possible to be 'United in Stupidity,' 'United in Arrogance' and 'United in Hatred.' 'United' has a negative as well as a positive potential, and Ralph Waldo Emerson illustrates this very well in his essay on 'Compensation.' Surely, there is good and there is evil. There are pluses and there are minuses in all of creation."

"Why do you think this is so?" asked Anderson.

"It has much to do with Adam," replied Peter.

"So now the Garden of Eden myth!"

"You might want to hold up a bit on the fashionable business of dismissing the wonderful and forceful *biblical* story of the Garden of Eden as a myth, silly and ridiculous. 'Realists,' apparently such as yourself and possibly most if not all of those who work with you in the vineyard of the *New York Times* as well as the rest of the news media, fail to see the Adam and Eve story for the mysterious and rich allegory that it most likely is."

"*Pilgrim's Progress?*"

"What about *Pilgrim's Progress?*"

"It's an allegory."

"Yes, it is, in that Bunyan's literary effort symbolizes mankind's torturous journey toward the celestial light."

"How is the Adam and Eve allegory different?"

"Well, for one thing, since you've brought it up, the Garden of Eden account in Genesis is an allegory symbolizing mankind's tragic journey *away* from the celestial light."

"The question is, it seems to me," said Anderson, "Should I take a leap of faith that the Garden of Eden story is more than allegory, that in fact it is real? Yet having said that, it gives me a huge problem with the theory of evolution."

"Fair enough. I am also an evolutionist."

"Oh?"

"Of course. Evolution also means 'development,' and it means 'progress.'"

"*Pilgrim's Progress?*"

"Yes. A human-written allegory to explain a biblically written allegory to make God's mysterious truth more understandable."

"So there *was* a Garden of Eden."

"Of course there was, just as there was really an Adam and an Eve and a fall from grace and a need to recover it."

"I think I'm seeing it," said Anderson.

"Let me ask you this," said Peter. "What have you to lose by believing that there *was* a Garden of Eden?"

"Only my soul," said Anderson.

"Then you do see it. You are a good student, Mr. *New York Times*!"

"Do you have a definition for *soul*, Mr. Pence?"

Peter P. Pence worked the tip of his shepherd's crook along the crack in the floor near his feet. He folded his lips inward and felt the pressure of his teeth against them. He worried the growth of his beard on the right side. He looked directly into the eyes of Robert Anderson. Finally, Peter spoke:

"*Soul* should not be rigidly defined. Since I am human as you are human, body-bound as you are body-bound, I have earthbound limitations. I believe I have a soul, and I believe that it lives both in this mortal, aging bag of bones, and will live forever outside what you presently see. I believe my soul will live eternally in Heaven or Hell, and I believe I have an earthly responsibility to marry good deeds with good faith and submit myself to God's judgment as to whether in His eyes it is good enough for me to be welcomed in his Home."

"Mr. Pence, I'm not at all sure that this part of the story I'm doing for the 21st century edition of the *Times* will make it into print."

"You mean..."

"The cutting room floor."

"I understand this, and the implication is that the 'cutting room floor' has validity and the news managers are the best judges of what is important. However, they will 'get theirs,' as Emerson has promised in *Compensation*."

"Excuse me?"

"There are many 'cutting room floors.' Your newspaper's is only one, and in fact, much of what your editor considers 'All the news that's fit to print' may very well wind up on Peter P. Pence's 'cutting room floor.'"

"I can't wait to tell Charlie."

"Charlie?"

"He's my editor. He thinks he's God."

"Oh, my. But there's nothing new or unusual about the shenanigans of journalists, bullfighters, messianic megalomaniacs and other preposterous creatures."

"That's Charlie."

Back when he was 30 years old, Peter P. Pence was still the owner of 100 shares of Amalgamated Copper, 100 shares of Union Pacific and 100 shares of Standard Oil (adjusted for stock splits, of course). True, he had anticipated the stock market crash, had sold enough of his portfolio to build Angel's Rest without a mortgage, had already paid off his brother Robert's college debts, yet it was something else that he'd done that he was convinced had shaped his life for the next 70 years: he had obeyed the eleventh, twelfth, thirteenth and fourteenth commandments. He had invested in the ideas of the humanities by saving his money and adding to his collection of books, keeping his daily journal and faithfully recording the collective dream of his parents, Patience and Prudence, his grandparents, Jacob and Suffiah, Daniel and Armilda, and his great-grandparents Chad, Jessie, Jeremiah and Lucy Ann.

CHAPTER NINE

T he red bulb on the telephone was flashing when Robert
Anderson emerged from the shower at the Starlite Motel in
Crossland, Kentucky. He hated the flashing red light with a growing
passion, because it usually meant one thing. The *Times* was calling.
Anderson, wrapped in a towel a little too small for his paunch, water
dripping down the middle of his back, dialed the numbers for New York.

"I've looked at your last fax," said Charlie.

"And?"

"I think you're going overboard. Does this dude also handle snakes?"

"Charlie, you're a certified, card-carrying, sonofabitch, hound of Hell."

"Listen, Martin Luther, Billy Sunday, whoever in the hell you think
you are, let's remember what we're doing here. We are *not* saving souls."

"You wouldn't know one if it stung you on top of the head."

"Anderson, I'm telling you. The story is a 100-year-old man who
lives in the boonies and that's pretty much it."

"Look, Charlie, you're the editor. You're in charge of the cutting
room floor. Be my guest."

"You're damned right, I'm in charge here, and your story is not the
only one in or out of town. Keep it simple, stupid. Wrap it up and get the

hell out of the Pocket or wherever it is you're holed up. By the way, what's her name?"

"Suffiah."

"Suf-what?"

"Armilda."

"Anderson, damn your soul."

"Prudence. Her name is Prudence," Robert Anderson shouted.

"Anderson, go to Hell."

"I'll probably see you there," said Robert Anderson as he slammed the phone back on its cradle. He dressed and drove back to the Pocket to keep his weekly rendezvous with Peter P. Pence. Anderson talked with himself as he drove past a small, sagging barn that once had been a shelter for new dreams and plans for the future.

"Charlie's right...you're becoming involved...you shouldn't become involved...you know damn well you shouldn't...but it can happen...it has happened before...you get this urge to be a human being, you know?... you get this urge to stop the car and start rebuilding old, droopy barns... you want to see life in them again...you want to see somebody, anybody, maybe a kid, maybe a young woman, maybe an old man, just somebody in the barn milking a cow, burying a head in her flank, turning the teat and giving the cat a squirt full in the face...you want the walk to the barn, and you want the walk from the barn...you want the fullness of the stars and the moon hanging there, easing into its next stage...you want to stop the words and just fill the air with breath...you want to feel your feet meeting the earth...you want the warmth that comes from opening a door and stepping inside."

Robert Anderson often struggled with himself, using it as a way of pushing ahead, taking the next step, trying not to look back, but always to see what was around the turn in the road. He had come to terms with the idea that ultimate truth was *always* just around the corner. When he came to the foot of the hill beneath the dogtrot, he sat for a brief time, then turned off the ignition, stepped outside the car and slowly began walking to meet with his old friend.

"Mr. Pence, may we discuss the meaning of wealth?" Anderson asked.

Peter took the old Bible from the table, and he read from St. Matthew, Chapter VI, verses 26-29:

> *"'Behold the fowls of the air: for they sow not, neither do they reap, nor gather into barns; yet your heavenly Father feedeth them. Are ye not much better than they?'*

> *"'Which of you by taking thought can add one cubit unto his stature?'*

> *"'And why take ye thought for raiment? Consider the lilies of the field, how they grow: they toil not, neither do they spin.'*

> *"'And yet I say unto you, That even Solomon in all his glory was not arrayed like one of these.'"*

"Mr. Pence, ever since I was a child and first heard these words in Sunday school, I have had a problem with this idea."

"It is another allegory. You should have no problem with ideas expressed through allegories. Of course, you and I must sow and reap and gather into barns. You and I choose not to run around without clothes. You and I have human toil to perform and sometimes that includes spinning. My mother, Prudence, and her mother, Armilda, and her mother, Lucy Ann, took deep satisfaction in spinning clothes for their families to wear. The imprints of their hands and feet will never be erased from the spinning wheel, which my great-grandfather Jeremiah built for his Lucy Ann, the same spinning wheel handed down to me."

"So, help me with this allegory, please."

"First of all, an allegory, as we have agreed, is a word picture that *represents* an idea. The passage from St. Matthew, I believe, is telling me to sow my seed as intelligently as I am able, reap its abundance as industriously as possible, and gather it into the barn with care and planning. In time I will parcel it out as thriftily as possible. There is no reason for me to have a second barn or a chain of barns. One barn serves my modest and honest needs."

"On the other hand, you never married and if the species were depending on your seed for true wealth, it would be sadly lacking, which it is. Mankind needs the progeny of a Peter P. Pence."

"I accept that as a genuinely proffered compliment, and I think it deserves an explanation. No man can do everything. No woman can do everything. It is true that I would have been most pleased to have fathered a child. It just didn't happen. I didn't marry, because I valued my solitude too much. Perhaps that makes me selfish. On the other hand, if I had *only* fathered children and had not fathered thoughts, had not fathered understanding about all the things that you and I have discussed, then my parenting might have been as vain and insignificant as Longfellow's 'dumb driven cattle.'

"And it would be better if there were less parenting among the thoughtless," offered Robert Anderson.

"We should never attempt to play God," replied Peter. "When we start doing that we wind up in a dark swamp."

Peter returned to his Bible: "As for raiment, I will be sufficiently warm in winter and cool in summer, but I will not dress ostentatiously. I see no point in having two coats when one will do. I will not have three pairs of shoes when two will do. I will not wear ties that are wide this year and narrow next year. I will not own an automobile."

"You've never owned an automobile!" Robert Anderson said, incredulously shaking his head.

"I'm tempted to ask you why you think I *should* have owned an automobile, but since we've declared a truce on the issue of my asking you questions, I will tell you why."

"Thank you."

"I have never owned an automobile, in fact I don't have the foggiest idea as to how to drive one, because I've never believed that it has ever made the slightest bit of sense for me to be *going* anywhere. Remember Finster's Law of Location..."

"Wherever you go, there you are."

"Exactly. I don't deny that automobiles lie at the heart of our national machinery, 'progress,' as it's called. And maybe I was not 'patriotic' when I spurned the Lizzy after which my brother, Adam, lusted. I simply turned my passion toward intellect, chose instead to adorn my mind with improved thinking. I will resist all temptations to think fashionably. It will be my life's work to think with as much originality as possible."

"How and when did your original thinking about originality occur?" Correspondent Anderson asked as he made a check mark in his reporter's notebook.

"Perhaps it came in a copy of the first major literary work I ever owned: *The Adventures of Huckleberry Finn*. For me, it was Huck's innocence, honesty and courage that piloted him and Nigger Jim out on the Big River. They were fleeing the artificialities of their captivity by using their natural abilities and headed for freedom."

"*Huck Finn* has been pulled from many library shelves."

"Yes, I know, but I see no difference in this than I do burning a book. It's all the same. It's censorship, and I abhor it," replied Peter as he walked to the wall lined with his vast collection of books.

"And yet," Anderson countered, "these times of political correctness exact a certain toll, a price that should be understandable to one as compassionate as you, Mr. Pence."

"I assume that '*Nigger* Jim' is the problem," the old man replied.

"Yes, if you were to sum it up in one word that would be it," Robert Anderson answered. "That word has become highly offensive to a large segment of our society, and it has become not unlike shouting 'fire' in a crowded theater."

"Words are sounds that represent thoughts, nothing more, or should be nothing more. 'Nigger Jim' was a term of endearment to Huck Finn. Huck didn't want to enslave anybody. He didn't know the meaning of hate. He was caught in a time when slavery was an established system in the United States of America, as it had been in many parts of the world for centuries, including Africa. To pull this classic from library shelves for this reason alone is to miss Mark Twain's point altogether."

"Which was?"

"Two human beings on the Big River, one Black, one White, in a relationship of trust and caring, and love."

"But..."

"Young man, you asked about my ideas concerning *wealth*, I believe. Here," said Peter P. Pence as he drew an arc with his right arm, "here is my real wealth."

"Your books?"

"I never throw one away. I certainly would not burn one, for there is no warmth worth that price. As Milton said: '*As good almost kill a man as kill a good book: who kills a man kills a reasonable creature, God's image; but he who destroys a good book, kills reason itself, kills the image of God, as it were in the eye.*'"

"The *Areopagitica*," said Robert Anderson. "I have loved it since a professor in college caused me to read it for the first time."

"And I have stocked my shelves with books as carefully as I have stacked firewood in summer for consumption in winter. I don't consider it a prideful thing, but I especially love leather-bound books with handsome paper and gold-tipped pages and fine fabric page markers. Thus they are substantive when held in the hands by the fireplace, the warmth of the wood for the body, the warmth of the books for the mind."

"What is the range of the books?"

"Limited, yet at the same time boundless. My intellect draws mainly upon the American experience. I have not studied Greek or Latin. The British gave up on the likes of me about the time of Tom Paine's *Common Sense*. The heart of my collection is preserved in the Franklin Library's '100 Greatest American Masterpieces.' *Huck Finn* is one of the 100. So are my other favorites: Crane's *The Red Badge of Courage*; Dreiser's *Sister Carrie* and *An American Tragedy*; Emerson's *Essays*; Frost's *Complete Poems*; Hawthorne's *The Scarlet Letter*; Howells' *The Rise of Silas Lapham*; Longfellow's *Poems*; Melville's *Moby Dick*; Norris' *The Octopus*; Sinclair's *The Jungle*; Steinbeck's *The Grapes of Wrath*; Stowe's *Uncle Tom's Cabin*; Thoreau's *Walden*; Warren's *All the King's Men*; Whitman's *Leaves of Grass*; and Wolfe's *Look Homeward, Angel*.

"I have indulged myself by investing in the *Oxford English Dictionary* set with its companion volumes, and from time to time I reach back beyond my favorite, *The American Heritage Dictionary* of *the English Language*, yet the primary source for the development of my intellect, such as it is, and such as anyone might think of it, has been my own *intuition*. There is simply no substitute for the real thing."

"Current newspapers, magazines, radio, television, movies—they have no place in your education?" the man from the *New York Times* asked.

"Very little. The *Times* is an important exception. It has been my college education. Too often the media are a hideous waste of time. As Thoreau said, the report of one train wreck should suffice one's morbid curiosity."

"Mr. Pence, would you have all Americans in the year 2000 living as Thoreau did at Walden Pond?"

"No, I would not. In fact, as Thoreau declared, I will not presume to tell *anybody* how they ought to live, but at the same time I devoutly hope that everybody else will leave me alone to live as I choose. My connection with Henry David Thoreau is not as direct as his with Ralph Waldo Emerson, but I too aspire to continue the tradition of what Emerson described as 'The American Scholar.'"

"What do the teachings of Emerson mean today?" Anderson asked.

"Have you read his essay, *Self-Reliance*?" asked Peter P. Pence.

"No."

"Have you read his essay, *Compensation*?"

"No."

"Then your education can hardly be said to have begun. I won't say you must read these priceless works, but I'm tempted to say it. I believe it is best for all individuals, of course, to make their own discoveries. But it will not be without criticism from religious dogmatics, who see grave errors in the transcendentalism of Ralph Waldo Emerson and the raw individualism of Walt Whitman and Henry David Thoreau."

"Mr. Pence, upon your recommendation and no other I will read

Emerson's *Self-Reliance* and *Compensation*. May I read them here in the quiet of the dogtrot?"

"Indeed you may, but before you begin to do that, I should like to ask you to meet with me next Friday evening, rather than Sunday. You see, just past midnight on this December 31, New Year's Eve, I will become 100 years old. The sand in my hourglass is running out quickly. Although I don't expect to see a burning bush, or to receive a token as did my good father, Patience, I know I don't have a precious moment to waste. Besides, I have a bit of a surprise for you."

"Shall I be here about 6 o'clock?"

"That will be fine."

Robert Anderson prepared to leave and drive back to Crossland.

"Mr. Anderson, I should like to ask you a personal question, even though I know that you don't like me to do that. Consider this one a heartfelt, personal inquiry."

"Sure."

"Mr. Anderson, are you happy?"

"I don't know how to answer that. It really depends on what you mean by the word 'happiness.'"

"Here's what I mean," said Peter. "I mean are you now at this time in your life doing the thing that matters most to you in every respect? Can you truly say that you do not wish to be doing anything else? Can you truly say that you feel so fulfilled that were you to see the burning bush this very moment, you would be willing to be consumed by it without any regrets, without any remorse, without any reservations?"

"Is it confession time?" asked Robert Anderson.

"If you choose to call it that," replied Peter.

Anderson sat down on a nailkeg and said, "The truth is, I know what I'm doing is most incomplete. I know it is filled with compromise. I always harbor a feeling that there is something else I should be doing. I know I am not living up to my fullest potential. Sometimes I feel as if there's a large hole in the bottom of my bucket, and the water is always running out. Other times I feel as if I'm like a dove riddled with the blast of a shotgun, and a know-nothing hunter puts his foot on my lovely dove's head with my eyes pleading, and tries to twist it off. Oh, yes, the Charlies of the world are forever taking a bead on me."

"The Charlies of the world?"

"Charlie, my editor."

"Wouldn't it be better if you became your own editor?"

"Doesn't work that way."

"Shouldn't it?"

"Probably."

"So, do it."

"How do I begin?" asked correspondent Anderson.

"I have an idea," said Peter.

"Yes?"

"It is part of the surprise. See you next Friday?"

"I'll be here," said Robert Anderson.

CHAPTER TEN

"Well, Mr. Pence, I feel as if I've received an education from you, as well as a very fine story for my newspaper," Robert Anderson said as he met with Peter P. Pence on that cold and snowy Friday, December 31, 1999.

"Your education is not finished."

"Another commandment?"

"No, but an invitation, which you may find strange."

"I can't imagine turning down *any* invitation from you."

"Perhaps you should wait until you hear what it is. You see, as I said when last we met, tomorrow is my 100th birthday," he said with dignity and pride.

"Congratulations, Peter P. Pence. I'm sorry that it has taken me so long to know you and have you for a friend."

"You have nothing for which to be sorry. Even if you had known me for years, you might not, probably would not have had quality time for me. I would have forgiven you for it. You see, no one anymore remembers my birthday, haven't for many years. I can't remember the last time anybody remembered it. I do not feel as if I've been forgotten. Yet, I shall not forget. Nor shall I forget my dear parents. Each

December 31, no matter the condition of the weather, I go to be with them. This year I'm inviting you to join me."

"I'm sure you can understand that I do not understand."

"Perfectly."

"Cause me to understand, please."

"I have two sleeping bags. One for you and one for me. Should you be willing, I would like you to join me this evening at the family burial place up on yon hill."

"Of course, I'll join you. But, why will we be needing sleeping bags?"

"We will be spending the night together at the burying place."

Robert Anderson took a deep breath. His brow tightened. He smiled and replied:

"After all I've learned from you in the past eight weeks, Peter P. Pence, I cannot imagine anything more interesting than to spend New Year's Eve with you at the family burial place. I am deeply honored that you would want me to join you and to commemorate your 100th birthday. But are you sure you will be able to do it? It is cold outside, and the snow is continuing to fall. There may be six inches on the ground by tomorrow morning."

"Time is on my side. I have nothing to fear, except fear itself. Didn't Franklin Roosevelt say that? No matter, a long time ago I forsook fearing fear. There is no fear in me. There is no place for it. Why should I allow fear to occupy a cubit of space within me? Fear is the work of the devil. I do not love God by being fearful, although it has been written, especially in the Old Testament, that God is wrathful, 'Vengeance is mine, sayeth the Lord.' It is also written, John XII, verse 24: 'Verily, verily, I say unto you, Except a corn of wheat fall into the ground and die, it abideth alone: but if it die, it bringeth forth much fruit,'" concluded Peter P. Pence.

The reporter and the old man headed out through the doorway and their feet made crunching noises in the new-fallen snow.

Peter took his time, holding the tightly rolled sleeping bag within the arc of his left arm, his right hand clasping the tall, hardened, cedar shepherd's crook. His woolen headpiece rested on the bank of his eyebrows and doubly protected his neck above the collar of his lamb's wool coat.

They walked together without speaking until they passed the barn with the corncrib built with the logs of the Rock Ledge church house and at last, silence did not seem possible.

"About 200 years ago," said Peter P. Pence. "About 200 years ago."

"Mr. Pence, I shall never forget the irony of that church becoming a corncrib. When you first showed it to me, I was saddened. But then I thought it was funny. Now I'm back to being sad again."

"The building itself was not important. It was the people, the foolish people who spent too much of their money on 'foreign' missions and not enough on themselves."

"Mr. Pence, perhaps sometime we might talk about the dangers of isolationism."

"Xenophobia?"

"Yes."

"It is not that I distrust foreigners, Mr. Anderson. All I'm saying is that if we don't put our own house in order first, we will be unable to help any outsiders."

They headed on up the hill, taking their time, feeling the connection of their feet with the whitened and crystalled earth, sparkling with the snow that continued to fall in flakes large enough to catch on the warmth of their tongues.

"Who tore the church down?" Robert Anderson asked.

"My father, Patience."

"Weren't there any objections?"

"Oh, no. Nobody wanted it. Nobody wanted to keep it from falling down after the small congregation began to scatter. New churches were built in nearby towns, and of course many of them are gone now, too."

"May I ask you how much he paid for the old church building?"

"He offered $10.00."

"They accepted?"

"Yes."

"A handsome price at that time."

"Oh, yes, and a 1908 Indian head Gold Eagle it was, too."

They reached the top of the hill where the snow had almost covered nine stones. The reporter and the old man lowered their sleeping bags to the ground, and using his gloved hand Peter P. Pence brushed the snow away from the stones. Anderson bent closer to watch the names appear.

"There are no names. This stone marks the place where my brother Paul has been sleeping for 117 years. This stone marks the resting place of my father. By his side, beneath this stone is my mother. Next to her is where I will be," Peter said as he turned to pull the binder twine to open his sleeping bag. "The other stones are in memory of Jacob, Daniel, Suffiah and Armilda."

"Would you like me to use a limb to clear away the places for our bags?"

"Yes," said Peter. "You'll find over in that locust thicket the wood for starting our fire too. If you'll be so kind as to do that, I have the matches for the warmth we shall share."

Robert Anderson went to the thicket three times, returning on each trip with a good armload of small locust logs, which had been stacked there in a neat woodpile. He also brought a limb shaped much like a rake.

"I have the idea that somebody has been working to keep that woodpile replenished."

"Yes, that has been one of my pleasures. Shall we light the fire?"

"You bet."

Peter P. Pence took from his greatcoat three dry corncobs with the brittle husks still attached at the base. He fanned out the husks of one of the cobs and placed it on the ground next to the stone above his mother, Prudence. Then Peter took two country kitchen matches and struck the sulphur heads against themselves. When the miniature burst of flame appeared, Peter quickly brought the stems of the two matches together, gingerly touching the fire to the waiting corn shucks. They in turn began to burn, heating the dried cob, spreading the flames upward. He took the second cob and laid it against the first, waited a few moments for the fire to grow, then added the third cob.

"Would you like to join me now in adding some locust twigs?" he asked.

"Thank you," Anderson replied as the warmth of the flames reached his fingertips and seemed to spread slowly inward.

"You see," said Peter, "everything worthwhile is the result of a process, a nurturing procedure. Hardly anything of lasting significance, good or bad, occurs instantaneously."

"My generation is guilty of thinking so."

"Yes, and that is probably the heart of the problem of many preceding generations. It was Paula's problem, Adam's, Poplar's, and Paul's, although he was not old enough to understand the cause of the cholera that robbed his life. But, the disease was a process too, working its way back and forth through this part of the country in four epidemics. It was not until Paul had been dead for ten years that a German scientist positively identified the bacteria responsible for the disease. Many had died before that time, before *their* time. And there were preachers who kept insisting that it was neither sanitation nor bacteria that were the cause."

"God's wrath?"

"Oh, yes. It was payment for sins committed, they said."

"Then it is surprising that more in your family did not die of cholera."

"Don't make me angry again with your mockery, young man, but yes, many of my ancestors did die of it, although sin didn't have anything to do with it. There were people without sin who also died of cholera in 1832, 1849, 1866, and 1876, and there were many in the Pocket who did not escape the horrifying deaths. Paul was infected after most people, even the medical experts, had wrongly judged that the problem had been solved once and for all. Simplistic thinking. Nothing could have been further from the truth."

The fire was catching now and Peter P. Pence and Robert Anderson sat by the side of it, feeling its warmth against their faces. Orion, the

Great Hunter of the heavens, had stalked his path, slipping low over the hills to the east. The Big Dipper and the Little Dipper with the North Star were on their stations.

"Mr. Pence, how did your mother and father deal with religion?"

"The kind found in the old Rock Ledge Church?"

"Yes."

"They were afraid of it. But, they didn't know what to do about it. So, they mostly stayed away from it. They lived, without knowing it, in the spirit of Ralph Waldo Emerson."

"Relied upon themselves?"

"And the Bible."

"Your mother, Prudence, read to you from the Bible?"

"And my father. It was something we always did at the end of each day."

"But why would your father buy the logs, the flooring, siding, the skeleton of the old church and bring it all to his farm to build a corncrib?"

"It was good wood."

"Are you now joining me in mockery?"

"No, not at all. It *was* good wood, and it certainly was worth one Gold Eagle."

"He must have felt *some* irony in converting a church into a corncrib."

"A church *building* into a corncrib. Buildings should not be confused with people, my good friend. Nor should windows and flooring be confused with matters of the spirit. Let's see if I can do a better job of explaining. Two years before his death, my father saw an opportunity to invest in hand-hewn log beams. The walnut pews had been ripped out and sold to antique dealers. Nobody knows what happened to the handsome lectern. I hope it is on somebody else's farm, turned on its side and used to store shelled corn. For the most part, this church's roof had fallen in, what windows there were had been broken. Patience really just wanted the log beams."

"Do you mind if I unroll my sleeping bag and slip inside it?" Robert Anderson felt cold enough to ask.

"You're bored with my prattle."

"No, I'm not, not at all."

"Then I think I shall unroll mine too. It's also too cold for an old man like me."

They lay in their sleeping bags while, near their faces, the small fire befriended them. The flames sounded satisfied as they consumed the large snowflakes drifting earthward. The air was pleasantly still.

"What do you suppose happened to the $10.00 Gold Eagle?" Anderson said at last.

"What generally happens to all such coins?"

"Wasted?"

"Of course. Consider the Liberty-Draped Bust half-cent piece of 1800. From what I understand, there were two issues of that coin in that year and now one (in what they call "fine" condition) is worth more than $10,000. Even the first Lincoln cent, minted when I was 9 years old, has increased in value 50 times over."

"That is a different matter, scarcity, as in rare coins, I mean."

"Is it really?"

"Maybe not. Did you hear about the guy in Ohio who saved 8,000,000 pennies over his lifetime?" Anderson asked.

"News fit to print?" chided Peter P. Pence.

"Yes, well, there was this guy who began saving pennies when he was five years old, saved them all of his life. About five years ago he turned them all in to the bank—barrels of pennies worth an estimated $80,000."

"Were there any rare pennies among them?" asked Peter P. Pence.

"They said they were too busy at the bank to spend the time to find out."

"Exactly my point."

They stared into the flames and watched descending snowflakes, some as large as pennies, dissolving upon contact with the heat. Anderson watched the face of Peter P. Pence and saw sadness in his eyes. He returned the look, and he smiled at Anderson.

"Mr. Pence, at midnight it will be your birthday. It is now ten minutes away. I've brought you a present, something I thought would please you. It's a small coin, a freshly-minted 2000 Lincoln-head penny."

Anderson extended his hand across to Peter's. He took the miniature velvet pouch containing the new penny, and as the New Year began, the reporter and the old man saw to the west of them a display of fireworks.

CHAPTER ELEVEN

As the new day began to soften the darkness, the full moon sinking in the west, Robert Anderson awoke to find Peter P. Pence adding more wood to the fire.

"It lasted through the night?"

"Embers," he replied. "You blow on sleeping embers to start new fires."

"Thank you for the best New Year's Eve party I've ever attended, and happy birthday," Anderson said as he propped up his head with his hand, rubbed his eyes and stared into the flames. "Do you realize, we're now in the 21st century?!"

"Yes we are, and I have a gift for you. I also have a request," said Peter.

The *New York Times* correspondent listened, as a rooster began to crow down by the corncrib built of the logs of the old Rock Ledge Church.

"I have no one to whom I would rather entrust my fortune than you. Of course, it is not too much by some standards, but it's probably a great deal more than most are ever able to accumulate. It includes the house, the barn, and 100 acres of land, and that is the most important part in addition to the principal to which last night I added your gift of one freshly-minted 2000 Lincoln-head penny."

"Mr. Pence, I am honored, of course, but you shouldn't be doing this. Are you sure there is no one else you'd rather have accept this gift?"

"There is no one."

"I hate to ask, but I must—how large is the principal?"

"About $1 million."

"Oh, no. Oh, no. This is crazy," Robert Anderson whistled and shook his head.

"As I said, the $1 million itself is not as important as the land, which is priceless, and equally precious is the process by which the bottom line was earned."

"You are a remarkable person, Mr. Pence."

"You must promise me that you will do everything within your ability to protect the principal and the land."

"Mr. Pence..."

"Please don't speak, not yet. Permit me to finish. You came to me in the beginning wanting to know the secret to the accumulation of my wealth. I have shared that with you. Now, on my 100th birthday, on this day that I will die, I want you to take 10% of the principal—$100,000— and I want you to create a chapel, a very small chapel, within the corncrib. The crib should be surrounded by a building of natural stone— no stained glass windows. It will become a place for prayer. It should not be a place for preaching, therefore it will not be necessary to employ a preacher. Let the preachers come to pray too if they wish. Therefore, it should be simple. No statues of saints, please. There should be a walkway from the road, where, I suppose of necessity, there will have to be a dry and reliable parking lot. We wouldn't want any 'Lizzies' to become bogged down, would we?" he said with a laugh.

"And the dogtrot, it will be preserved," Anderson said, almost feverishly, as he rolled up his sleeping bag. "Your leather-bound books will be catalogued and made available for reading."

"Will you come each New Year's Eve to tend the fire?"

"Yes, and I'll invite someone to walk to the burying place, and we will talk and sleep there to greet another New Year."

"I hope you will exchange new pennies."

"Anything more than that would be pretentious."

"How will you allocate the $900,000?" asked Peter.

"I won't *spend* one penny of it. Anyway, it's not mine, it's ours and I'd invest it in the establishment of a new school, where students are taught the ten commandments and the eleventh, twelfth, thirteenth and fourteenth commandments, and I would name the school after you, Mr. Pence. I would call it 'The Peter P. Pence School for Living.'"

"That would not be necessary," said Mr. Pence.

"It might not be necessary, but that is what I would do, but what name would you give the chapel, Mr. Pence?" Robert Anderson asked.

"How about Saints Prudence and Patience?" he replied.

"Oh, my goodness, yes!" the *New York Times* correspondent exclaimed.

"My parents were not saints, but they were as good as any I know. I think they and my brother Paul deserve to have their names and years added to their stones, don't you?"

"Yes, I do. And what should be on the stone above you, when that sad day arrives?" Anderson inquired.

"My name, Peter P. Pence, and my years, 1900-2000."

With strong and strange finality, the old man said the numbers, 2000, and Anderson looked into his eyes and feared the message blazing there, almost as if in a burning bush.

"Mr. Pence, are you all right?" Robert Anderson cried.

Peter P. Pence clinched his fists tightly and raised them high above his head, not in defiance but in victory, not in despair but in delight.

"I love you, Lord," he said, and then, taking one deep breath, he fell to his knees. Anderson hurried to Peter and lowered him to his side. Placing his fingertips on the sides of his face, Anderson felt a slow, irregular pumping. With both hands, the reporter scooped up snow and placed it on the fire, and with tears streaming down his face, for a moment he looked into the eyes of Peter P. Pence, who seemed to be methodically slipping away.

Robert Anderson opened Peter's right hand, which held the velvet pouch for the new penny, then closed it again. He thought of trying to carry the old man down to the dogtrot, at first dismissing it as an impossibility, then knowing it was something he must do. Anderson could not leave him in the snow while he went for help. Coydogs might find him. Anderson raised Peter's body up and positioned it on his back by grasping his wrists with his hands, then stumbled back to the dogtrot.

There was nothing to do but to place the old man in his rocking chair. Correspondent Anderson would tell the authorities that he had died there, for he knew no one would believe that they had spent the night at the burying place. He also knew that no one would believe the story about the gift of $1 million. In fact, Anderson had no idea where all the money was kept.

"Mr. Pence, where is the money? How will anyone believe me when I tell them of your wishes?" he whispered to the ashen face.

"The nailkegs," whispered the voice.

"What about the nailkegs?" Anderson asked.

"The nailkegs where we've been sitting...they're filled with silver dollars. The other nailkegs...they're filled with pennies."

"Mr. Pence, for God's sake, Mr. Pence!"

"Key to the safe-deposit box," said Peter as he fumbled to loosen the chain around his neck. He handed the chain and the key to Anderson, then reached inside his shirt pocket and drew out a piece of paper. "My handwritten will. Names you executor of all I have."

"Don't talk any more, Mr. Pence. Promise me that you will not say another word. I'm going to my car, where there's a mobile telephone. I'm calling for an ambulance."

The first call was to 911.

The next call was to Charlie at the *Times* in New York City.

"Charlie, listen to me."

"Where the hell are you?"

"I'm at the dogtrot in the Pocket. There's an emergency."

"What the hell...?"

"Peter P. Pence is going to die, so shut up and listen to me. We spent the night at the burying place. Not long after I woke up, Mr. Pence told me he was going to die. He collapsed. I carried him to the dogtrot. I put him into his rocking chair. He told me I was to be the executor of his estate."

"You're a goddamned reporter and don't you forget it. Your ass belongs to ME."

"Charlie, you're wrong, wrong, wrong. I USED to belong to you. You're going to have my story, but I'm not coming back. I'm staying here and you can go and take a royal flying leap."

"Listen, Anderson..."

"No, YOU listen. There's a fine old man here who's probably going to die on his 100th birthday. He needs me. You don't need me. The final draft of the manuscript will be faxed to you this afternoon. Take it or leave it."

"Anderson..."

Robert Anderson hung up the telephone and walked back toward the dogtrot. He was relieved that the first day in the 21st century would be his last day with the *New York Times*. It had been a good career. It had been filled with excitement. There had been the coverage of the civil wars in Central America. There had been space shots, the second landing on the moon, the voyage to Mars, volcanic eruptions on earth, hurricanes, presidential campaigns, mass murders, political assassinations, but never before and maybe never again had there been or would there be a Peter P. Pence.

The thumping sound of a helicopter came nearer and the chopper appeared, a speck above the trees on the western slope of the homestead carved out of the woods by Jeremiah.

As Anderson approached the form in the rocking chair he knelt down and looked into the old man's face. There was a peaceful expression there. "Help is on the way," said Anderson. "They'll be here any minute now. Where is the rest of the money?"

"See Malcolm Davenport, the president of the bank...the bush is burning..."

"Mr. Pence..."

"The bush is burning...going home to be with Patience and Prudence...one day you will join us?"

"Mr. Pence..."

Peter P. Pence's last words were followed by a drawing in of a deep breath. The expiration of it was long and smooth. Footsteps sounded in the dogtrot. The medics entered and hurried oxygen to the side of the rocking chair, where Peter sat with his head tilted down.

"He's gone," said Robert Anderson as he stepped back and allowed the medics more room. "He's gone," repeated Anderson as he walked back outside the dogtrot and stood for a time looking down toward the corncrib.

"He's gone," said the medics. "We'll take him in, but he's gone. Radio the coroner."

The burial of Peter P. Pence alongside Jacob, Daniel, Suffiah, Armilda, Patience, Prudence and Paul was a short service, following a visitation in the corncrib. The casket was open, because Peter had specified it in his will:

"...To me, it is important that people see my face and be able to touch the sleeve of my coat. I want those who come to say goodbye to be certain that I have lived, and I have died, and that this time will come to all and that no one should feel ashamed or afraid. The earthly meaning of my life I have entrusted to Robert Anderson, and to him will pass the responsibility for spreading the word about material and spiritual wealth. I pray the message will be heard and heeded, for unless this occurs, I am far less certain about the survival of the United States of America in the 21st century. While all my earthly treasure is now in the safekeeping of

Robert Anderson, all my spiritual treasure remains with me and God our Father."

"Grandfather," said Samuel, as he and Robert Anderson stood alone at the burying place after the last shovelful of dirt had been placed in the grave, "thank you for making it possible for me to meet Mr. Pence."

"Samuel," said Anderson, "thank you for wanting to meet him."

"Do you suppose I might be like him?"

"He would be very disappointed if you didn't at least try."

"I'm sorry my mother and father could not have been with us today. But, they're busy, I suppose."

"Just about everybody is busy, Samuel, and that is a part, maybe a very big part of the problem. Too many of us are running harder, yet still slipping behind. That's why it is so important to remember the value of a single penny. It means working for it, saving it and allowing it to grow. Mr. Pence, our good friend who now rests on this hillside, so loved Ralph Waldo Emerson that he might well be saying to the two of us right now: 'Nothing can bring you peace but yourself. Nothing can bring you peace but the triumph of principles.'"

Robert Anderson and his grandson stood in silence for a time, and then they walked back down the hill. The neighbors and friends of Peter Pence had departed for their homes. The American flag was fluttering on the edge of the dogtrot, and the wind chimes were playing their own version of an anthem for Peter P. Pence. Back upon the hill, at the burying place, Pumpkin was mournfully howling.

When Robert and Samuel approached the front steps of the dogtrot, the figure of an old man moved slowly around the west corner. He appeared to be quite elderly, and he walked carefully with a cane. His hat was slanted slightly to the left side with a hint of stylish intent, and the shoulders were sloped forward as if closet-worn, a tired place for a musty coat to hang. The old man's left hand was in the coat pocket, the thumb hooked outside. He stepped closer to Robert Anderson, and looked directly with eyes as green as a cat's, nothing to hide, and no turning back from the prey of the moment. There was a strong resemblance to Peter. Robert Anderson was stopped dead in his tracks. A strange feeling of fear swept through Anderson as the man began to speak.

"The name's Pence."

Robert Anderson stiffened. He instinctively took Samuel's hand and firmly held it.

"My father was Adam Pence."

"Samuel, why don't you go inside and find something for Pumpkin to eat?" said Anderson.

"Maybe Old Uncle Peter told you about my father. I'm sure he did."

"Mr. Pence..."

"I'm not here to make trouble. Not here asking for anything. When I heard that Old Uncle Peter had finally passed away, I had my grandson drive me down from Cincinnati. That's where I live. That's where I've lived the whole 90 years of my life. Guess we kind of missed the funeral, didn't we?"

"Yes, sir, you did," said Anderson, tenuously.

"It's not too late to sit down for a little while, is it?"

"No sir, it's not too late for you and your grandson to come inside for a little talk."

"We don't want anything," repeated Mr. Adam Pence.

"I understand that," said Robert Anderson. "We'll offer you a little southern hospitality. You'll accept that, won't you? Come on in. My name is Robert Anderson, and that was my grandson, Samuel. Watch those steps, we're going to do a little work on them."

"My name is Adam Pence III," said the middle-aged man, who helped his grandfather up the steps of the dogtrot.

"Ever been here before?" asked Robert Anderson.

"No, sir, we've always managed to stay away. Great-grandfather Adam was the black sheep of the family, as I'm sure you know, and we never felt comfortable about coming here."

"Well, then," said Anderson, "have your grandfather sit awhile in his Uncle Peter's rocking chair, and we'll become better acquainted. You sit on that nailkeg, and I'll sit on this one, and Samuel can sit on the edge of the fireplace.

"You will probably know soon enough," said Robert Anderson, "I've been designated executor of the estate."

"We would not have come," said Adam Pence III, "if my grandfather had not believed it was time to pay respects. Ironically, it's the week of his birthday also, but I know it appears that we must resemble buzzards."

"Not at all. In fact, I'm delighted that relatives of Peter are alive and that there's no break in the blood connection with this place, where in the future many others will be making pilgrimages to discover the value of the penny and what it can mean to them as individuals, to the nation and the world."

"Mr. Anderson," said Adam Pence, the elder, "My grandson and I don't have the slightest idea what you are talking about."

"You don't know about your Uncle Peter's beliefs concerning the penny?"

"We always figured he was close with his money, if that's what you mean. Mr. Anderson, I grew up in an orphanage, had no idea who my parents were until I was a grown man, steaming and shaping hats on Vine Street in downtown Cincinnati. One day, a man comes in to pick up his fedora. When he heard my name called out—'Adam Pence'—the customer said, you wouldn't happen to be related to the Pences of Kentucky would you? He said he was descended from the Dr. Pence who was well known in Cincinnati. That was the first indication of who my father was. I never did find out anything about my mother. As for the side of the family going back to the famous Dr. 'Pine' Pence, we never connected up. They were the upper class, and we were somewhere in the middle.

"You say you stayed in Cincinnati all your life?"

"Yes, sir, I did," said Adam, rubbing his hands along the armrests of Peter's chair.

"Raised a family?"

"Raised a family. Seven sons. Now I have so many grandchildren and great-grandchildren, can't keep 'em straight. My first son, Adam II, investigated our side of the family tree. He discovered the truth about my father and shared it with me before he died. He was killed in the first wave at Normandy Beach. He was 18 years old, and he never saw this only child of his."

"Mr. Pence," Anderson said to Adam III seated on the nailkeg, "Are you interested in tracing family connections?"

"Yes, I am, and I've always looked with fascination upon the name, 'Peter P. Pence.' I'm ashamed to say, though, that he was never a real person in my life, because most of us in the Eden area of Cincinnati were raised up on the idea that all Kentuckians were hillbillies, and the last thing anybody wanted to do was to admit that there was a connection."

"You're familiar with the Pulitzer prize-winning play, *Kentucky Cycle*?" asked Robert Anderson.

"No."

"It's just as well. The Academy Award-winning movie, *Forrest Gump*?"

"Yes."

"Well, the reference the next day after the awards ceremony was: 'A story about a nitwit southerner.' No one would say, 'a *nitwit* from Cincinnati,' a 'nitwit from Iowa' or a 'nitwit from South Dakota,' yet all three places have their abundant share of nitwits."

"Mr. Anderson," said Adam Pence from Peter Pence's rocking chair, "What happens next here, in the Pocket, in Kentucky?"

"I've resigned from the *Times*, and I intend to be the curator for the Peter P. Pence School of Living. I'll also be the custodian for Saints Patience and Prudence Chapel."

"You'll live off Uncle Peter's estate?" asked Adam.

"Not an unfair question," said Robert Anderson. "I have my retirement from the *Times* and I have income from my free-lance writing. I'll also have a small social security check. To answer your question, and I don't blame you for asking it, as curator and custodian, I will do everything within my capacity to be sure that the wealth accumulated by Peter P. Pence will be saved for the next 100 years, and, God willing, the next 1,000 years."

Robert Anderson addressed Adam Pence, III: "Have you any idea what you're sitting on?"

"Looks like a nailkeg."

"Yes, it does, but it doesn't have nails in it. It's filled with silver dollars. And this 'nailkeg' I'm seated on—it's filled with silver dollars."

The young Adam Pence remained seated as he felt the sides of the nailkeg, lightly touched the fine, wood splinters of it. He tried gingerly to rock back and forth on it, but it was quite heavy.

"Silver dollars?" he asked.

"Yes, and there's more, much more. Your Uncle Peter spent a lifetime working—hauling crushed rock, splitting rails for fences, caning bottoms for chairs, which he had made with his own hands and his own tools—reading the *New York Times* for over 50 years, investing in the stock market, but most of all saving his pennies. Some he converted into silver dollars. It is my responsibility to see that each penny of the wealth of Peter P. Pence be saved and used as he requested."

"Well, I'll just be damned," muttered the elder Adam Pence.

"No, saved," replied Robert Anderson with a smile. "You see, there're many things here greater than pennies and silver dollars, and it goes far beyond all the books accumulated by Peter during 100 years of living. Were he here, your Uncle Peter might be speaking for St. Mark: 'For what shall it profit a man, if he shall gain the whole world, and lose his own soul?'"

The older and the younger Adams and Samuel waited for Anderson to continue.

"There's much work ahead both here and out of the Pocket, but the greatest thing of all, I believe, is the message left by Peter P. Pence to the people of his country he loved. That message includes the Ten

Commandments and the eleventh, the twelfth, the thirteenth, and the fourteenth commandments, which he created and practiced all his days."

"Mr. Anderson," said Adam Pence, "My family is God-fearing. There is nothing unusual about us. Most of us have worked hard all of our lives to have what we do. We pride ourselves in owning our homes. We don't make trouble. We fight in wars when our country says it needs us. Adam the III is nearing retirement as an infantry Master Sergeant. He survived Viet Nam.

"I'm just past 55 years old," said Adam III.

"Why don't you take retirement? I certainly could use your help here at the dogtrot. This place needs a Pence!"

"Let me think about it," said the younger Adam. "Yes, let me think about it. I have a wife, but our children are all grown." There was a lengthy pause. "Something tells me, Mr. Anderson, we need you more than you need us."

"All relative. All relative. Just as long as we can work together. Just as long as we can keep intact the principal of Peter P. Pence. Just as long as we can educate others to practice and cultivate new principles, we will have done our part for our nation as it moves on into the new century."

"Mr. Anderson," said Adam Pence III, suddenly, "you got yourself a deal!"

EPILOGUE

I n the year 2010, upon the tenth anniversary of the passing of Peter P. Pence, Samuel, who soon would be 21 years of age, arrived at the dogtrot in the Pocket. He parked his car at the foot of the hill and walked with his girlfriend, Lucile, to the corncrib.

There were many states represented by the license plates on the cars in the graveled parking lot. The path up to the shrine for Patience and Prudence was filled with people politely stepping aside for others to pass.

"The quiet was awesome," said a young woman who looked to be about 30 years of age.

"Yes," replied her male companion as he smiled at the approaching younger couple.

Samuel guided Lucile to the limestone building containing the corncrib, and hand-in-hand they stepped inside. They sat on a simple walnut beam with notched, pegged legs. The high noon sun pierced small, unstained windows around the domed top of the structure, and the spokes of light set Lucile's long, fine-combed hair to shimmering. Samuel put his arm around her shoulder and inclined his head toward hers. They sat in silence for a long time and there was no counting of minutes. Lucile cupped her hand on the side of Samuel's face, warmth flowing from her fingertips, and he placed his hand upon hers, sealing the connection.

Samuel wept.

The young couple, who planned to be married in the chapel the following month, walked to the top of the hill—to the burying place. They stood by the headstone for Robert Anderson, placed there in 2005. Samuel had seen to it that the engraver included the word, "Journalist." He'd considered the possibility of "Pulitzer Prize Winner" but had dismissed the idea as quickly as it had come.

There were simple markers for Adam Pence Jr. and Adam Pence III.

"Samuel," said Lucile, "I am very sorry that you and your grandfather did not have more time together."

"We had enough...more than enough," said Samuel."...It could also be said that Peter P. Pence and I did not have enough time to talk. Time—like money, like love, like a trusting relationship with God—should not be always measured simply by quantity. Even though Peter Pence amassed a fortune, and even though my grandfather acquired a wealth of contentment, it was the splendor of a few precious moments, just like a few precious pennies, that really mattered."

Lucile placed stems of jonquils by each of the gravestones, then she and Samuel—the new curator and custodian—turned and walked back down the hill to the dogtrot.

ACKNOWLEDGEMENTS

I am grateful for the preservation of spoken words arising spectrally from the Perryville battlefield, where today there is a museum and annually there is a commemoration of the fighting that occurred there on October 8, 1862. I am also indebted to George W. Grider and Norman H. Franke, authors of the essay, "Pharmacy, Medicine and the Battle of Perryville, Kentucky," as well as Hambleton Tapp's "The Battle of Perryville, October 8, 1862, as described in the diary of Captain Robert B. Taylor" (the diary is in the Library of the Kentucky Historical Society, Frankfort). Other invaluable sources include: the enormously detailed United States Government's *War of the Rebellion*: *Official Records of the Union and Confederate Armies, Vol. XVI*.

The continuing encouragement of the Kentucky Historian Emeritus, Thomas D. Clark, is gratefuly acknowledged. His volume, *Pleasant Hill and Its Shakers*, based on the research of F. Gerald Ham, is a rich source for accounts of the days immediately preceding and following the tragedy at Perryville. Dr. Clark's *Historic Maps of Kentucky* has likewise proven to be invaluable.

The theological counsel provided by Father John Madden of Lexington, Kentucky, and the Rev. Charles Dietze of Henderson,

Kentucky, is acknowledged with deepest gratitude. They are good, sensitive, compassionate souls, who were always willing to be sounding boards without forsaking their own beliefs.

Kentucky artist Jackie Larkins of Harrodsburg has sensitively captured both the agony of the fictional Prudence and the proud individualism of her son, Peter. Jackie's talent grows, yet his personal kindnesses remain a constant joy.

Thanks to the designer of the cover and the typesetter, Stacey Freibert, and proofreader/editor Carole Boyd, for their painstaking work, without which this volume would be formless.

Finally, my deepest gratitude to the chief editor of all I do, my wife, "Lalie," without whom, in mind and in body, I would be penniless.

David Dick
Plum Lick, Kentucky
June 2, 1995